ST. AUGUSTINE

ST. AUGUSTINE

by

JACQUES CHABANNES

translated by

JULIE KERNAN

DOUBLEDAY & COMPANY, INC.

GARDEN CITY, NEW YORK

Excerpts from *Saint Augustin et La Fin de La Culture Antique* by Henri I. Marrou are used and translated by permission of Editions E. de Boccard. Excerpts from *Histoire du Bas Empire* by Ernest Stein are used and translated by permission of Desclée de Brouwer & Cie.

CONTENTS

ST. AUGUSTINE

Chapter One

CHILDHOOD
354–370

Patricius Herculus rode his mule sidesaddle with a dignified air. Since he was a member of the "very honorable municipal council," that is to say, a decurion and therefore a full citizen of the Roman Empire, he had the right to wear the toga. In the days when he wore the short tunic of a "subject" he willingly bestraddled the mule. From certain points of view that posture gave him better balance as he rode the pebbly roads of the nearby mountains. Now, however, Patricius found it incompatible with his dignity as a Roman citizen.

Despite his forty-six years he was virile and black-haired, and ably guided his animal through the steep, narrow streets of the old city. Tagaste (today Souk-Ahras) had increased in size under the Roman ordinance. It was on the road between Hippo (Bône) and Madaura and halfway as the crow flies between Carthage (Tunis) and Cirta (Constantine). The new quarters of Tagaste had houses several stories in height, as in Carthage and Rome; they were built in a straight line the length of the streets which opened onto the main highway running from the sea to the mountain. But the ancient Moorish village was still perched high on its small peak, and there Patricius had kept his old family dwelling. He loved the upper city with its little houses, the *mapalias* of uncut stones piled one upon another, looking like boats with keels in air.

Nestling in a forest of yew trees, Tagaste was huddled on a plateau between three peaks of the mountain, the highest of which was defended by a fortress. Narrow streets climbed up clay banks that had been ravined by the torrential winter rains. The white houses shone in the morning sun, and between them could be seen glimpses of the soft blue sky of Africa.

On this day Patricius had reason to be in good spirits. The night before, his wife, Monica, had given easy birth to a second son. Monica was a fine wife and a good mistress of his home. To be sure, she was a little too Christian; she indulged in proselytism and wished to convert her husband. Patricius resisted. Even if the emperors nowadays were Christian, one never knew. Besides, many of the big property-owners remained pagan—perhaps as guardians of the ancient beliefs and out of gratitude to the gods. Patricius admired them.

In addition, there was the schism of the followers of Donatus who had broken away from the Catholics and formed a separate Christian sect in Africa. Should one be a Catholic or a Donatist? Every city had two bishops who excommunicated one another. Was it any wonder that under the circumstances Christians did not know which sect to follow?

Patricius was distrustful and preferred to wait. "Wet your finger when the wind blows, as they say; then you will know what you have behind you." Patricius had no intention of preventing Monica from making the sign of the cross on the forehead of the newborn child, as was the custom. It would do the infant no harm, especially since his father would place offerings on the altars of Venus Genetrix and Ceres, so that these two goddesses would protect his little son. Patricius always carried on his person small packages of sulfur, a frog's leg, and cabalistic formulas to which he added, in order to please Monica, a parchment envelope containing prayers. It was the best use he could make of them, for he did not know how to read.

As for the rest, he would wait as long as necessary to make sure of being on the strongest side at the right moment. There was no hurry.

Patricius was a little brown man, swarthy and with quick black eyes. He could be irascible, even brutal. His appetites were violent and demanded instant satisfaction so he could go on to other things. But he respected his wife. Much younger than he, she imposed this respect by her distinguished ways and her austerity, which chilled him somewhat. He never struck her, even if he often deceived her, while she, on the other hand, seemed completely indifferent to the infidelities of her impetuous spouse.

Other matrons with more attentive husbands were often beaten. Monica considered it proper to close one's eyes to the disorders of men and to hold one's tongue when they became angry. She explained it thus: "You have been told once for all that you are your husbands' servants. Do not rebel against your masters."

Patricius was content with his lot despite his worries over the unpopular functions assigned him by the municipality. He was responsible for the collection of taxes and under the administration of Emperor Constantius II defaulters were given short shrift. When he wished to gather the *annones* (taxes in kind, wheat, grain, cattle) in order to pay the mercenary armies and also a part of the salaries of officials, Patricius often had to have recourse to armed force.

The fiscal laws went even so far as confiscation of property, and the new *curiale*, recently arrived from Carthage, was without mercy. For instance, death duties reduced an estate by half, and one could no longer sell a slave or a piece of land without authorization. The members of the municipal council had to be able to withstand the fury of the taxpayers on the one hand and the anger of the *curiale* on the other.

As the owner of some land (*possessor mediocris*), Patri-

cius supervised his own property, gave careful attention to his
vineyards, his orchards, his wheat fields, also to his slaves,
among them the pedagogue charged with his children's education. He often said: "I am neither a Phoenician nor a
Numidian, but a Roman. I have the fighting spirit of the
Numidians and the Phoenician shrewdness, but my administrative ability comes from Rome."

That day as Patricius crossed the marketplace he received
the Roman salute from the buyers and even from a number
of the nomads. In order to continue, he had to force his way
through a mob of these people swathed in the ample folds of
their white woolen garments and to avoid the neighing horses
and the lowing oxen, all surrounded by swarms of biting black
flies. Important Roman citizens passed, followed by their
retinues. The copper-skinned nomads advanced slowly amid
the crowd of black slaves and gaudily dressed, gold bejeweled
prostitutes and the fortune-tellers who exorcised demons and
claimed to possess cures for sickness. Negro dancers turned
and whirled until they were ready to drop from exhaustion;
the wind whipped the animal skins in which they were clad,
and as they danced, they beat with muffled strokes on their
enormous drums. Here and there could be heard the whining
melody of a little mandolin made of tortoiseshell and
stretched hide.

This was a Mediterranean city, clamorous, picturesque and
alive, a customers' market where the peasants came from
great distances to buy and sell. Here they encountered a new
world—the grandeur of Rome. Quickly perceiving the comforts it offered, they wanted them for themselves. All they
saw excited in them a desire for gain and hence for work—a
desire not natural to men and especially not to Mediterranean
men.

In Tagaste they sold cattle from Aurès, dates and hides
from the Saharan regions, grain and wine from the plains.
The city was also the bazaar to which the nomads came to
seek provisions to carry home. Their taste for buying grew

and their needs multiplied as they gazed on the merchandise offered for sale.

In the new city were ultramodern baths, paved with mosaics and adorned with statues; there was a theater and a forum. The triumphal arch, the pride of the inhabitants, was made of four marble columns with crowning capitals; the niches between contained handsome statues. The wide sidewalks, reserved for pedestrians, were overhung by balconies giving protection from the sun. Here and there gushed fountains, providing water for travelers' steeds. Behind the colonnades opened up the shops, each containing a great marble table on which the merchant displayed his wares. Around each of these pressed a crowd.

Patricius rode out beyond the city. It was hot but the air was healthful, and Tagaste could count some inhabitants over a hundred years old. The Roman road from Carthage to Cirta, built on a cement bed covered by large, regularly aligned stones, branched off at Maragaira. This secondary route went as far as Hippo Regius where another road, leading to Chellaba, began.

The countryside was very pleasant and might be described as a greener, a better-watered Galilee. To the traveler from the rocky regions of Cirta or the great arid plain of the Medjerda, these valleys seemed gaily opulent between the mountains covered with pines and cork trees, abounding in small game and birds—pheasants, quail and thrush—as well as large animals such as the wild boar.

From east to west stretched vast wooded areas, valleys and rushing waterfalls. To the south could be seen several bare peaks with pointed cones. Here the cows grazed in the meadows. There a plow, drawn by a little donkey and a slave, harnessed side by side, bore its sharp harrow into the hard and rocky soil.

The river Bagradas, coming down from the Aurès, wound its way across the fertile plain, its waters available to the peasants for their fields. The entire region had been put under cultivation and the price of land had tripled since the Romans had brought in abundant water and now purchased all the African wheat for consumption in the big cities of Italy. North Africa had become the granary of Rome.

Each piece of property was crisscrossed by countless irrigation ditches. Because in the greater part of the plain the inhabitants had the river water at hand, orchards and vegetable gardens had grown in number. There were communal oil presses within the villages, and those who raised olive trees, vineyards and fruit trees were exempt from taxes.

At that period could be counted around Madaura and Tiaret as many farms and villages as existed sixteen centuries later in the entire north of France.

The oldest race of North Africa was the Berbers or Moors (Kabyles, Ruaghas and Tuaregs). Even before the Romans came, the Phoenicians had conquered and enriched themselves upon this region.

Similar in appearance to the Egyptians, these Moors were wide of shoulder and narrow of hip; they were short and dark, energetic and nervous. When Sallust was governor of Numidia, he tried in vain to discover the remote origins of these Medes or Moors, these nomads or Numidians whose predominant characteristic was restlessness. Vergil spoke of the African shepherd who, bringing with him his dog and weapons, his tent and his flocks, "wandered about in the desert solitudes" for months at a time.

Nevertheless the Kabyle-Berbers had become farmers, anchored to the soil by the Roman proconsuls. Due to the proximity of forests and springs the valleys had become very fertile, and the Kabyle-Berbers had been taught to raise wheat. In accordance with their usual practice, the Romans had wooded the mountains with such success that soon they were sending cedar and oak overseas. (All these riches were to dwindle during the Vandal occupation and after the arrival of the Turks and Arabs were to disappear entirely, giving place to arid mountains and desert brush.)

Immense aqueducts and cascades were constructed, and in the cities fountains gushed into the little basins placed beneath them, so that one could hear the light refreshing sound of splashing water which the Romans loved so well. From these basins the water ran off into troughs and was distributed to the homes of the citizens for their private uses.

The original language of the Kabyles was related to that of the Saharan Tuaregs. Many of them had interbred with the Phoenicians, especially in the cities. After B.C. 146, the year when Scipio Africanus burned Carthage, the native rulers had become vassals of the Empire. Septimius Severus was born in Africa, as was his son Caracalla. When he later became emperor, he conferred the rights of citizenship on all freemen born in those African territories which had been organized into municipalities. All immediately felt the strong attractions of Roman civilization and citizenship and proudly inscribed on their tombs the words *Civitatem Romanam Consecutus*—One Who Achieved Roman Citizenship. As soon as they had the right, they cast aside the short tunic and woolen cloak of the natives and donned the Roman toga. They took Latin names, as did Augustine's father, Patricius. Many became officers and functionaries, occupying more and more important posts in the Empire. Their sons rose to the senatorial rank.

Thus Rome made its conquest of their minds and hearts. For their part, they contributed to the Empire's greatness and prosperity. Africa furnished two-thirds of the wheat consumed in Rome, not to speak of olive oil and cattle. Rome covered North Africa with roads, cities and monuments, traces of which are still to be seen on the coast. (A Roman law forbade exiles to enter African ports because they would have found there "the same pleasures and language as in Rome.")

The Roman State knew, therefore, how to rule, and it imposed on the African people its language and customs, and then its religion. It organized its veterans into colonies and distributed to them uncultivated land. Citizenship and exemption from taxes were granted to retired soldiers, even those of barbarian origin.

Unfortunately, after the beginning of the fourth century, Rome passed through a severe crisis for which historians give many causes. Among these were:

An absurd fiscal policy.

An idle population living on provisions distributed free: professional nonworkers.

A centralization of power which was totalitarian in character.

A declining birth rate due to love of easy living.

An officious and parasitic bureaucracy.

A menacing class struggle.

The impossibility of increasing exports.

The degradation of the civic sense of citizens who ceased to take interest in public matters in order to look after their personal affairs. (Romans no longer believed in the greatness of Rome.)

The Senate's loss of all power and control. The Senate had been the last barrier in protecting the State against the imperial whims.

Local posts no longer attracting first-rate men, but only traffickers avid for personal riches.

The growing number of barbarian mercenaries—Goths, Visigoths, etc.—in the Roman armies.

The withdrawal of Gaul and Britain from the Empire when they elected emperors of their own.

The barbarians taking advantage of insolvent Roman policies in the economic as well as moral and social domain, and opening the gate to the West.

The lack of gold and silver in the State treasury. Money no longer had its proper value but only a value arbitrarily fixed by the State.

A constant rise in prices over a period of fifty years coin-

ciding with the devaluation of money. (The inflation under
the Emperor Gallienus amounted to ninety per cent.)

Taxes in kind (bread, wine, oil), obliging the peasants to
pay not only these levies but also for the transport of their
produce.

The loss of the divine status of the emperor when Christianity was adopted officially.

A constant war between emperors and usurpers to the
throne (there were six emperors in the year 307).

Nevertheless, for many centuries Rome had cast her light
upon the world and had given a modern meaning to the
word *civilization*. She had recognized the right of holding
property, created and increased industries, had modeled her
rulings on a true distribution of power, had long administered
the Empire with a justice unparalleled in history. She had
built up an incomparable culture, educated the people, constructed solid roads and cities on a practical plan, had built
aqueducts, hospitals, universities, planted trees by hundreds
of thousands if not by millions, invented central heating,
and spread her magnificent language throughout the world.

What had happened that the worm had entered so far into
the fruit?

By A.D. 350, Rome had ruled Carthage for five and a half
centuries. The Mediterranean was a Roman lake: *mare
nostrum*. But Constantius, the son of Constantine, had to
put down three successive attempts to usurp his power, and
to defend Roman Africa foot by foot against Julian, his cousin.
Besides this struggle, the territory suffered violent repercus-
sions from the upheavals in every other part of the Empire.

Christianity had gained a stronghold in Africa more than
a century before, at the cost of the lives of many martyrs.
Tertullian, the first of Christian African writers, has de-
scribed their cruel deaths in the circus, the beheading of
Bishop Cyprian, the ground bestrewn with Christian blood.[1]
But if Christianity had gained in Africa, its unity had

been difficult to maintain. Schisms proliferated, among them Arianism and Donatism, against which Augustine was to struggle until the end of his life. There were other heresies. Manichaeism especially, originating in the East, had become strongly rooted. It was to make its way underground until the thirteenth century when Catharists and Albigensians rose to strangle the Church and nearly succeeded before they were definitively vanquished by the gentle stubbornness of Pope Innocent III and the miraculous Francis of Assisi.

Patricius was nearing forty when he married Monica, whose age was seventeen. Monica's forebears had been Christians for several generations and they too belonged to the Kabyles, a division of the Berber race. Saint Augustine sprang entirely from a stubborn stock, nurtured from remote times by the Mediterranean sun, real aborigines whose blood remained pure in spite of Africa's frequent invasions by other peoples.

Monica had been reared, according to the custom in middle-class families of easy circumstances, by an old slave who had been with the family since the birth of the girl's father and had "carried him on her back," when he was a child. A fervent Christian, this slave had witnessed the last of the persecutions in the region. Respected by her masters and loved by their children, she was nevertheless a very severe taskmaster, and under her rule the list of things forbidden was long.

When Patricius married her, Monica was strict in her Christian beliefs and practices. Her parents had decided on the marriage without consulting her, as was ordinary in those times. The times were hard and they considered Patricius, a man of substance, as a good match for their daughter.

His young wife's militant puritanism disappointed Patricius, who was much enarmored of her. The daily observances of Christian life displeased him and especially the requirements of certain of its commandments. Monica, reared in the discipline of the primitive ages, spent nights in vigil at the basilica, observed days of abstinence and observed faithfully many other pious practices.

Each Sunday she visited the cemetery, carrying to the dead she wished to honor, balls of chopped beef, bread and wine. As she sat among the graves, these provisions were unwrapped and piously eaten and drunk in honor of the martyrs. Such pagan customs were strongly rooted and were long to survive in North Africa.

Taking advantage of her husband's strong attachment, Monica tried to convert him, but without success. She nevertheless secured his permission to inscribe the names of each of her newborn children among the "catechumens." This meant the sign of the cross was made on their foreheads, the salt was placed on their lips, but they did not as yet receive the water of baptism.

Patricius and Monica's first child was a son, Navigius; then they had a daughter (who later became a nun in the diocese of Hippo). On November 13, 354, after five years of marriage, their third child, Aurelius Augustinus, was born. A little dark boy, puny and nervous, he was fed by the wet nurses among the family slaves.

"Lord, your consolation and your mercies have raised me up, as I have heard from the parents of my flesh. . . . On coming into the world, I tasted the sweetness of woman's milk."

He grew up in the women's quarters:

"I do not know whence I came into what I may call a mortal life or a living death. . . . The comfort of human milk nourished me. . . . At that time I knew how to seek the breast, to be satisfied with pleasant things, and to cry at bodily hurts, but nothing more. Later on, I began to laugh, at first when asleep and then when awake."

Monica reared her son carefully. He was her last and favorite child. With his quick intelligence, he was as restless and unstable in spirit as in health. Small, dreamy and uncommunicative, he yet astonished his mother by the violence of his sudden outbursts.

Everything in the world surprised and disquieted him. He wanted to understand everything, at no matter what cost.

"Little by little I perceived where I was, and I wished to make my wants known to those who could satisfy them. Yet I could not do so, because the wants were within me, while those outside could by no sensible means penetrate into my soul. So I tossed my limbs about and uttered sounds, thus making such few signs similar to my wishes as I could, although they were not like the truth. When they would not obey me, either because they did not understand or because it would be harmful, I grew angry at older ones who were not subject to me and at children for not waiting on me, and took it out on them by crying. . . .

"I advanced from infancy and came into boyhood. . . . Yet infancy did not depart: for where did it go? Still, it was no more, for I was no longer an infant, one who could not speak, but now I was a chattering boy. I remembered this, and afterward I reflected on how I learned to talk. I myself, with that mind which You, my God, gave me, wished by means of various cries and sounds and movements of my limbs to express my heart's feelings, so that my will would be obeyed.

"However, I was unable to express all that I wished or to all whom I wished. I pondered over this in memory: when they named a certain thing and, at that name, made a gesture toward the object, I observed that object and inferred it was called by the name they uttered when they wished to show it to me. That they meant this was apparent by their bodily gestures, as it were by words natural to all men, which are made by change of countenance, nods, movements of the eyes and other bodily members, and sounds of the voice, which indicate the affections of the mind in seeking, possessing or rejecting things.

"So little by little I inferred that the words set in their

proper places in different sentences, that I heard frequently, were signs of things. When my mouth had become accustomed to these signs, I expressed by means of them my own wishes. Thus to those among whom I was I communicated the signs of what I wished to express. Thus I entered more deeply into the stormy society of human life."

Other than this, the child Augustine was filled with good will toward those about him and with admiration for the wonders of Creation. He had an early perception of man's dignity and of the importance of the person—of *his* person. This is the reason he was later to condemn with such violence the Roman methods of education, made even worse by their adaptation to Africa.

He retained a horrified memory of the real tortures to which children were subjected when they were slow to learn. The harsh methods they were forced to follow he described as "both toil and sorrow multiplied for the sons of Adam," and he called his teachers "executioners." What was worse, his parents gave him neither consolation nor comfort. On the contrary they "laughed together" when he told them of the constant floggings he received when he failed to read or write or to study his lessons. He was "horribly" beaten. And why? Because he was a little boy who liked to play and chatter. Yet he was chastised by men "who did the same things themselves."

When he was old, he wrote in his book *City of God:*
"Who would not shrink back in horror and choose death, if he were given the choice between death and his childhood all over again."

This shows to what point he was harmed, confused, and humiliated by these experiences. In his *De peccatorum meritis* he speaks with dismay of "the torpor in which we are enveloped, shrouded, in our early years."

"I was sent to school to acquire learning, the utility of which, wretched child that I was, I did not know. Yet if I was slow at learning, I was beaten. This method was praised by our forebears. . . .

"I prayed to You that I would not be beaten at school. . . . My punishments, which were then a huge and heavy evil to me, were laughed at by older men, and even by my own parents who wished no harm to befall me."

He never forgot this humiliation.

"I was beaten because I played ball. By such play I was kept from quickly learning arts by which, as an adult, I would disport myself in a still more unseemly fashion."

It was beautiful outdoors. The sun was shining brightly, the cicadas sang in the sweet-smelling pines. The woods around Tagaste were filled with nightingales, and the schoolmates who dared play truant amused themselves in the shade of the great trees. During this time the other pupils squatted on a rough mat in the whitewashed room of the *primus magister* (first teacher) and repeated in a singsong, monotonous chant the words and figures they must learn, all the while stupidly swinging their bodies from right to left and from left to right.

Augustine loved to play, especially when he was winner at the games. He and his companions fought mock battles between Greeks and Trojans, or they pretended to be gladiators or actors in a play. Augustine was early drawn to the theater, and after seeing a show would try "to imitate the frivolities" he had witnessed on the stage.

He liked to hear again and again tales and fables which excited his imagination and filled him with terror or exaltation. He was particularly fascinated by the love story of the ill-fated Dido and the Trojan hero Aeneas, who "wandered from place to place all over the world." (No doubt it was because Vergil had written the *Aeneid* that he was adopted by the Africans as their national poet.) Augustine learned Latin easily and naturally from hearing the language spoken—just as he had learned the Punic words at home.

From the teachers called grammarians he learned the laws of Latin and the mysteries of the poetic art.

"I was to speak Juno's words as she expresses both anger and sorrow because she could not turn back the Trojan king from going to Italy. I had heard that Juno never spoke these words, yet we were compelled to wander off and follow in the steps of these poetic fictions. . . .

"The men set up for my models were utterly dejected when caught in a barbarism or solecism while telling about some of their own acts, even though the acts themselves were not bad. But if they would describe some of their lustful deeds in detail and good order and with correct and well-placed words, did they not glory in the praise they got?"

Despite his distaste for the repetition of "one and one make two," his horror of the Greek language and his endless reveries about Dido, he proved a particularly gifted student.

"It was impressed upon me . . . that I might succeed in those arts of speech which would serve to bring honor among men and to gain deceitful riches."

His memory was good and he had a real gift of eloquence. Because of his proud nature, he feared the disdain of others, and most of all he feared ignorance.

Thus he reached his fourteenth year. The passing into adolescence was difficult for this passionate, sensual little Kabyle who stood anxiously on the threshold of a life that promised him both learning and pleasures.

The teacher perceived his superior intelligence despite his inattentiveness, his fits of anger, his whims and escapades. He advised Patricius to have the boy continue his studies in the humanities since, due to his frailty, he was obviously more fitted for the cultivation of the mind than of the soil.

Monica, always indulgent toward her youngest child (so delicate in health yet whose capabilities she vaguely divined), was quick to agree and to urge that the teacher's counsel be followed.

In the meantime, poor Patricius was having a bad year.

Politics was spoiling everything; the latest harvest could not be transported to Italy, with the result that the Romans were hungry and the Africans had no market for their wheat. Patricius had to make many sacrifices in order to send Augustine to continue his studies in Madaura.

At this time the Roman Empire, the colossus covering all of Europe, Asia Minor, Syria, Palestine and North Africa, had more than sixty million inhabitants. In addition, it did not know, even approximately, the number of its subjects among the barbarians living on its borders.

After the abdication of Diocletian, the executioner of Christians, and of his co-emperor Maximinian, Roman power was again divided, in 305. The Caesars Galerius and Constantius were promoted to the rank of *Augusti* and Valerius Maximinus and Valerius Severus were associated with them as Caesars and adopted sons.[2] Constantius, the first Augustus, received Britain and Gaul, Spain and northern Morocco; Severus was assigned Italy and Latin Africa; Asia Minor went to Galerius; and to Maximinus the other provinces of Asia and Egypt.

Maximinus and Severus had been chosen as Caesars to the neglect of the hereditary claims of Marcus Aurelius Valerius Maxentius, Maximinian's son, and of Flavius Constantine, the son of Constantius. The casting aside of these two sons of emperors was to have grave consequences. In 306, a year later, the Roman people, outraged by a new rise in taxes, rose in revolt and proclaimed Maxentius as emperor.

Maxentius ruled without great difficulty over Italy. He even figured as the restorer of Roman tradition and showed tolerance to the Christians. On the other hand, he had to deal with a revolt in Africa, for Maximinus, who had fought and conquered the Moors, counted many partisans in that region who refused homage to Maxentius. The result was that Africa had to pay for the luxury of an emperor of its own: the

Phrygian governor Domitius Alexander assumed the imperial purple and reigned for three years.

The rupture between Rome and the "wheat province" having had as its result a frightful famine in Italy, Maxentius decided in 311 to send a small army to Africa under the general Rufus Volusianus. Alexander tried to resist in vain. Cirta, the capital of the province of Numidia, where he had entrenched himself, was soon besieged and captured. Carthage was pillaged and sacked in turn.

Meanwhile in Rome an uprising of the people due to the famine was put down. This affair cost the lives of six thousand people, and the number of executions was increased in order to confiscate the property of the condemned. The barbarian mercenaries nursed their own ambitions as they kept a watchful eye on these conflicts between emperors and Caesars.

It was then that Constantine, who in his turn had been proclaimed Augustus on the death of his father Constantius in 306, assumed a leading role. In his struggle against Maxentius, his cousin, whom he considered an usurper, he began by denying any ties with the "Herculean" dynasty of Maximinian (this family of emperors, to authenticate their divinity, claimed to be descendants of Hercules, the son of Zeus). Constantine quickly invaded and occupied all of Spain, claiming this was in order to free the Franks. Next he made a surprise entry into Italy by way of Mount Geneva and marched on Rome, crushing Maxentius, who drowned himself in the Tiber (312).

Two emperors now remained: Constantine and Licinius (Galerius, Severus and Maximinus had died in battle or had been assassinated). Licinius was not a "descendant of Hercules," but had been Galerius' former comrade-in-arms. Cruel and bloodthirsty, although an able administrator, he was proclaimed Augustus in 308.

In 312, Constantine abjured paganism and declared himself a Christian. He soon incorporated the Church into the organization of the State, considering in fact that the welfare of the State was allied to that of the Church. Despite the resistance of the army, composed almost exclusively of pagans, he increased the power of the bishops. In many domains the Church was made the legal representative of the State, eventually being granted the right to receive inheritances.

Unfortunately at this time the Donatist schism broke out in Carthage (following the consecration of Bishop Caecilian in 311), and Arianism, another schism unleashed by Arius, a priest of Alexandria, gained firm footing in the East.

Briefly to give the background of Arianism we should say that at the time of Diocletian's persecution (around 305) a difference had arisen in Egypt between Peter, bishop of Alexandria, who had jurisdiction over the Eastern Church, and Meletius, bishop of Lycopolis, regarding the question of whether those who had apostasized but had repented could be received back into the Church after a period of more or less severe penance. Meletius favored a rigorous attitude in this matter and applied stern measures against Peter's advice. Because of this, his superior excommunicated him for insubordination. Later, however, many of the followers of Meletius were reintegrated into the Church and Arius was among them.

When the persecution of Christians was ended in 313 (Peter of Alexandria died a martyr on November 24, 311), a nucleus of Meletians still remained outside the Church, and they accused Arius of heresy. In a sermon Arius, who now occupied a leading role among the Catholic priests of Alexandria, had maintained that Christ was not equal "in substance" to God, but was the "creature" of the Father. The Catholic bishop Alexander demanded a retraction, but Arius refused. He was excommunicated and forced to leave Alexandria. Finding refuge in Asia, he rallied to his cause several Syrian bishops, including the celebrated historian Eusebius.

Under the influence of the Empress Constantia, wife of

Licinius, and Constantine's sister, two synods were held, one in Bithynia and in the other in Palestine, and both declared Arius to be orthodox. Immediately Alexander assembled a synod of one hundred bishops and induced them to ratify the sentence excommunicating Arius and his bishops from the Church.

Licinius, the second Augustus and emperor of the West and a foe of Christianity, rejoiced in this schism which diminished the power of the Church (under his rule Christians were banished from court and from army and administrative posts). It was due partly to antagonism in the religious sphere that a new conflict broke out, in 322, between the two emperors, Licinius and Constantine (they had fought earlier, in 314). Licinius was crushed in 324 and forced to submit to Constantine, who promised to spare his life but who had him executed shortly thereafter.

For the first time in forty years the Empire was ruled by a single Augustus, Constantine. He immediately revoked Licinius' measures against the Christians and wrote both to Alexander and to Arius urging them to become reconciled.

In 325, Constantine played an important part in the convocation of the first Ecumenical Council of the Catholic Church which met at Nicaea in Asia Minor. Its purpose was to reestablish religious peace as well as to define the relationship between temporal and spiritual powers. Constantine attended the sessions and followed the proceedings with great interest.

After the adoption of various important canons the Council took up the case of Arius and his disciples. A majority of those present supported Bishop Alexander; in fact earlier, at the beginning of the same year, a synod had been held at Antioch at which fifty-six bishops had condemned Arius' doctrine as heretical. In the first creed, or "symbol" of faith, adopted at Nicaea on June 19, 325, Christ was proclaimed *consubstantial* with God the Father, and thus Arianism was condemned. (In the form given this creed, in 381, at the

Council of Constantinople, it constitutes the dogmatic foundation of the Christian Church.) Although at Nicaea, Arius
and his writings were branded with anathema, his books were
cast into the fire, and he was exiled to Illyria, the heresy did
not die out and was to remain a source of strife within the
Empire for years to come.[3]

Around this time Constantine decided to build a city bearing his own name on the site of Byzantium and commanding
that strategic center of the East, the Bosphorus. The building of Constantinople was begun in 324 and the city was
dedicated on May 13, 330; it soon had 280,000 inhabitants.
Thus the survival of the Empire in the East was assured—
Constantinople was to outlive Rome for ten centuries as the
imperial capital.

After Constantine's death, the Empire passed through a
grave crisis. His sons divided the great emperor's powers
among themselves: Constantius II became ruler of the East;
Constantinus II received the West and had guardianship of
Constans, his brother, who was still a minor. When Constantinus II died (in 340), Constans succeeded him in the
West. A fiery young man, he halted the Franks on the Rhine
in 341 and reduced the power of the Arians by closing their
churches. He also took up the struggle against Donatism, the
schism which had sprung up in Africa and which had rapidly
assumed a political character. We will have more to say about
the Donatists in our next chapter, but must note here that
because they protected the "pillards," or highwaymen, and
the assassins known as "Circumcellions," they posed grave
threats to Roman order in Africa.

In 350, Constans was captured in Gaul by a military clique
which assassinated him in the church of a little village in the
Pyrenees. An officer of barbarian origin, Magnus Magnentius,
who headed the conspiracy, was proclaimed emperor by the
troops. Upheavals followed throughout the Empire, for Constantius set out to avenge his brother and rid the throne of

the regicide. In Italy, attempts at usurpation, coups d'état and massacres followed in quick turn.

From their base in Sicily, Constantius' troops took over Italy, but Magnentius held Gaul for an entire winter. Finally overpowered by the imperial armies, he committed suicide at Lyon.

In the meanwhile emperors, more or less sanguinary, with more or less fantastic claims, or acting as cat's-paws for others, rose up in every corner of the Empire. The duration of their power was often more or less ephemeral; for example, a certain Silvanus was proclaimed emperor by his soldiers at Cologne but assassinated shortly afterward. The Franks and the Alemanni took advantage of all this turmoil to make their stronghold on the Rhine.

The Empire was too vast and too turbulent for a single master. Constantius then decided to name his young cousin Julian, a military chief of real ability and a man of high cultivation, as Caesar for Gaul (355).

Augustine had just been born when Julian drove the Germans from central Gaul, brought the Alemanni in Swabia under submission, took Cologne from the Franks, straightened the Trajan line on the Meuse, and imposed reparations and levies in kind on the Alemanni in order to rebuild the cities they had destroyed and to maintain the occupation troops. Gaul was completely liberated from the incursions of these barbarians.

Soon Julian wished to be proclaimed Augustus and, to add to the strength of his position, he reinforced his army with Germans. Around this time Constantius II took measures to put an end to paganism and to destroy Arianism, which was gaining converts among the barbarians, but he died on November 3, 361, at the age of forty-four. On his deathbed he recognized Julian as his successor.

Julian, "the sole emperor," had become a militant pagan, having been initiated into the secret rites of Eleusis in 355. He ordered the pagan temples rebuilt, and, reversing the policy of his uncle Constantine, restored to the emperor the title of Heraclius. Christian functionaries were driven from their posts, the clergy lost all its privileges, and the Emperor proclaimed himself the high priest of the entire Empire. Taking up his residence in Antioch he began, in 362, a persecution of the Christians. It was, however, of short duration, for after declaring war on Persia, Julian was killed in combat, January 26, 363. With his reign, the line of Constantine came to an end.

Valentinian I was elected emperor by the troops at Nicaea in 364, and the following March, in Constantinople, his brother Valens was made co-Augustus. Both were Christians (they had to go into hiding during Julian's persecutions) and were the sons of Gratian, an army officer risen from the ranks. They came into power at a propitious time to divide the world empire between them without striking a blow. At Naissius in June 364, Valens became emperor of the East while Valentinian took the West and returned to Rome. They never saw one another again, and were to contribute to the rapid decadence and fall of the Empire.

Just as Augustine entered on life's stage, this disintegration began.

Chapter Two

YOUTH
370–374

Augustine had as a childhood friend the son of Romanianus, a wealthy and powerful noble. A Kabyle and the owner of vast estates, Romanianus was the leading citizen of Tagaste and presided over its municipal council. He dazzled the inhabitants of the little city with sumptuous entertainments, financing banquets on every occasion, arranging for combats between gladiators, bear fights and other amusements. Described as "the most humane, the most liberal, the most refined of men," he was also a bit of a snob, pluming himself on his culture and making a point of befriending poets and scholars. In Carthage too, where he maintained a residence in order to keep an eye on the export of his merchandise, he paid for spectacles of all kinds.

Romanianus lived at Tagaste in a magnificent marble palace in which he had private baths and other luxuries installed. Since it was again possible to send wheat, olive oil and wine to Italy, he was literally dripping with gold. Needless to say, he had an immense train of hangers-on.

He took a great liking to the little Kabyle with the piercing black eyes whose poetic leaning and sprightly conversation delighted him, and he decided to help his young protégé to continue his studies. So at Madaura, Augustine shared the comfortable lodgings that Romanianus rented for his son, Licentius.

Madaura was only about twenty miles from Tagaste on the road from Hippo to Cirta, a magnificent and much-traveled Roman highway running through the deep valley of the Medjerda. Louis Bertrand tells us that on this main artery "one passed long lines of chariots carrying provisions to the frontier garrisons, or the *annone* of the Roman people to the maritime port cities; or again, the palanquin or the mule of a bishop; or the curtained litter of a Roman matron. Suddenly at times all these would draw to one side of the road to make way for the passage, in a cloud of dust, of an imperial messenger." When the travelers had passed the forests, the old Punic walled city could be seen in the midst of a fertile plain watered by thousands of Roman ditches.

In Madaura, Augustine ceased to be a schoolboy and became a student. Now with greater physical freedom and able to take more initiative, he discovered a new world. The students were as rowdy and nonconformist as he could have wished. Madaura had many attractions; it was a real city and not an overgrown country market town like Tagaste. It could be proud of its past, for first of all it was the birthplace of Apuleius, the author of *The Golden Ass*, the philosopher, the wonder-worker.

The ancient city had a long tradition of culture, but also vaunted its modernity. Augustine and Licentius set out to explore it. To them it seemed grandiose with its public squares ornamented by pagan statues (two at least of the god Mars), its pillared temples and triumphal arches. The forum was vast and also filled with statues of every kind—of gods, demigods, famous citizens, emperors and philosophers. Apuleius, the local celebrity, was honored by the greatest number of statues of every kind and description and was regarded almost as a god.

Thanks to Romanianus and despite Monica's advice and laments—she had tried to warn him against the temptations of a corrupt city—Augustine frequented a society which,

mainly pagan, had revived and flourished since the reign of
Julian the Apostate. He took part in the feasts of Bacchus,
those wild and brutal carnivals in which no license was
considered excessive—which could also be said of many other
occasions, for the banquets in that prosperous city usually
ended in orgies. How could young Augustine, then at the
threshold of his fifteenth year, have failed to react with passion to the call of puberty?

He dreamed of love and soon occasions were offered him,
too searing to be described. He later confessed with confusion the troubles of this "uneasy adolescence":

"I dared to run wild in different darksome ways of love.
. . . Clouds arose from the slimy desires of the flesh and from
youth's seething spring. They clouded over and darkened my
soul, so that I could not distinguish the calm light of chaste
love from the fog of lust. Both kinds of affection burned
confusedly within and swept my feeble youth over the crags
of desire and plunged me into a whirlpool of shameful deeds.
. . . I defiled the very source of friendship by the filth of
concupiscence, and its clear waters I befouled with the lust
of hell."

He was nonetheless a good student, working furiously and
to good effect. Grammar, the first step in education, already
held no secrets for him. The fourth century was, in fact, the
golden age of *grammatica*, and Augustine was to remain a
grammarian all his life, with a pronounced propensity for
rhetorical forms, the use of copious anecdotes, definitions and
etymologies.

He was fifteen and happy to be alive, proud of his intelligence and the knowledge that he was admired, even respected, for his alertness of mind. As yet he had no other
thought, or so it would seem, than to study and enjoy life.
Into both he threw himself with passion.

Could one really say (with him) that he "became a real
pagan?" One does not believe this, for up to that time religion

does not seem seriously to have interested him.* Monica's devotion and passive piety appear to have had little influence over one to whom the first contact with life came as a desert wind, a sirocco of desires and sleepless nights. Doubtless, on the other hand, he resembled his father in more ways than one.

His teacher led Augustine to a wider understanding of Vergil, whose imaginative poetry he had loved as a child. He devoured the other Latin authors on the curriculum: Plautus, Terence—that subtle playwright and "honest man" (*Homo sum*); Seneca, Sallust, and Apuleius, of course; as also Horace, Ovid and the caustic Juvenal, and the earlier writings of Cicero. He studied these authors, in accord with the old Roman tradition, under four aspects: *lectio* (reading aloud, which included the teaching of diction); *ennaratio* (explanation of the text and literary commentary); *emendatio* (criticism of text and grammar, analysis of style); *judicium* (synthesis of the whole drawn from the earlier analyses).

He had also (without enjoyment, as he tells us) to study Greek, but relatively little. In Augustine's time the rift was growing which would break up the unity of the two Empires and separate the Greek East from the Latin West. This rift was to influence the whole of the culture of the coming Middle Ages, for the men of the West no longer grafted their expression on Hellenic modes of thought. Vergil had replaced Homer.[1]

Augustine forged ahead. By the time he was sixteen he had no more to learn from his mediocre teacher and embarrassed him with the questions he raised. He was bent on understanding everything and felt impelled to go further once he had understood. For him knowledge was a mountain to be climbed painfully, step by step, but once at the top he took

* [Yet at one point, St. Augustine says in his *Confessions* (Chap. 11) that when "still a child" he had been extremely ill and had begged for baptism; however, he had immediately recovered and his baptism was again delayed.—*Trans.*]

no time to enjoy the view spread out at his feet, for further on, a new and higher summit arose. Augustine would know no rest until he had conquered that height as well.

Already this intellectual mountain-climber was measuring his capacities. The idea of returning to Tagaste with his modest baggage of knowledge was unbearable. Why had he worked up so great an appetite for knowledge if it had to be left unsatisfied?

The teachers advised Patricius to send his son to Carthage. He had, they said, the makings of a rhetorician and it would be a pity if he did not pursue higher studies and become a lawyer or a teacher.

Monica was troubled by this and not at all in agreement. It was evident her son had contracted bad habits in Madaura and that his morals had been corrupted. It was high time for him to come back home.

Augustine returned, preceded by an established reputation for good scholarship and bad behavior. He had made up his mind not to remain long in Tagaste, for his aim, his dream was Carthage—Carthage with its culture, Carthage with its pleasures.

He lost no time in causing scandal in Tagaste, for soon he headed a little band of rowdy youngsters whose escapades could be condoned only by the indulgent Patricius. For example, one day they robbed a pear tree belonging to a neighbor (and elector) of Augustine's father, and threw the fruit to the hogs. At the same time many other misdemeanors were laid at their door, more or less deserving of heavy punishment. It seemed much ado about nothing to Patricius and he did not see that great harm had been done. The boys would have to grow up; it was only an excessive desire for youthful pleasure, he said.

One day when Augustine was at the baths, Patricius noted that his son had reached puberty. Coming home, he remarked with satisfaction that Augustine was now a man.

"From this, as it were, he already took pride in his grand-children, and found joy in telling it to my mother. He rejoiced over it in that intoxication wherein the world, from the unseen wine of its own perverse will, tends down toward lower things."

The good Patricius was delighted, for he thought that Augustine could marry and help him with his work. Patricius felt old age approaching and his eldest son, Navigius, was a good boy but unable to do much more than pass on orders to the slaves. If Augustine would marry, they would immediately give him a part of the land, and thus his living would be assured. He could teach grammar besides, if that amused him.

But Monica would hear no word of such a plan. Her viewpoint immediately and completely changed. Augustine must be sent away from Tagaste where he might take up with nobody knew what kind of girl, in view of his natural proclivities, and want to marry her. It would be better for the boy to go to Carthage and study law. He would win academic degrees and rise to an honorable position and thus could hope to make a fine marriage. For the moment he was only the half-instructed son of an honest small farmer. When he had the fine diplomas he could marry the daughter of a patrician—perhaps even Romanianus' daughter.

Patricius did not insist. Was this the same Monica who several months before had expressed such horror at the bare mention of Carthage? But how was anyone to understand women? Besides, Patricius was proud of his boy. He was a skinny little fellow, a dreamer, and filled with bizarre ideas, but perhaps he did have a real future! Only how were they going about setting up Augustine in Carthage so he could study there? There were many risks to be run in that city of perdition.

Finally recourse was had again to Romanianus, since it so happened that he owned a house in Carthage and often went there on business. He immediately agreed to put aside a

room for his young friend, for he held Augustine in real
affection despite the difference in their ages. He admired the
boy and believed he would one day become a celebrated
rhetorician—then Romanianus, his benefactor, would share in
his glory.

Monica, who still shrank at the mere mention of Carthage,
urged her son to curb his appetites. Was it not time for him
to be baptized so that he would receive divine help in resisting
temptation? Patricius, at the insistence of his wife (who assumed more and more authority in the household), had just
been enrolled among the catechumens. The time was not ill
chosen, for it now seemed clear that since the Emperor
Julian's death the pagans were definitely out of favor.

But Augustine was deaf to this suggestion and could think
of nothing but Carthage with its delights and opportunities
for learning. He expected everything of Carthage, perhaps
above all an answer to questions that haunted him when he
was alone and not inebriated by thoughts of poetry or pleasure.

He had embarked on a search and was avid for an answer. For sixteen years he was to carry on this quest with
growing anxiety, yet not once did he receive a reply which
would slake his thirst for truth and appease his hunger for
wisdom.

Carthage was one of the capital cities of the Empire, with
Byzantium, Antioch and Alexandria—and Rome, of course.
Augustine loved the wide streets, the temples, the beautiful
villas surrounded by shady gardens, the busy Mediterranean
port, the palm trees standing out against the sky, the city's
ring of forests and bright fields. He loved the heavy and
burning atmosphere rendered even more electric by the over-
whelming vitality of the people. Such was the new setting for
his amorous adventures.

Walking on the crowded streets was not easy. The pedes-
trian was jostled and harassed by beggars, bespattered and

covered with dust by horsemen, jostled and bruised by the soldiers who took up all the room on the sidewalks. Carriages were too numerous and in daylight hours were forbidden to use the narrow streets. The idlers among the Carthaginians walked about beneath the colonnades, exchanging news which they exaggerated and distorted in the course of repetition.

Like all Africans, the Carthaginians were gamblers. That was the reason the gaming houses were open only at certain hours and games of chance forbidden the rest of the time under threat of heavy penalties. But they played *micatio* in friends' houses, a game in which two players lift the fingers of the right hand, varying the number each time, and at a given signal each calls out the total number of fingers raised by the other.

The baths offered those who frequented them the most refined of pleasures—steam baths, tub baths, dry sudation, swimming pools. Around them were shops and gardens, massage rooms and halls for gymnastics. Here one could play three-handed ball, or *trigon*, with balloons filled either with air or with flour.

Public readings of literary works were held in the *auditoria* where the author-reader sat on a stage (wearing a new toga) facing his hearers, who sat on chairs or benches. Often these sessions drew vast audiences, since books, which were copied by specialized groups of slaves, were very costly.

On every street corner Augustine again found Vergil, his idol. The Africa of Dido and Aeneas was his Africa; one lived only by and for sensual pleasure. Captive princesses watched for their trueloves from the towers of mysterious palaces; in the meanwhile the gentle, perfumed prostitutes were waiting.

An unknown world opened up, and the life-force was present in extraordinary vigor. "You who went to Carthage . . ." Augustine, with nostalgia for his youth, was later to say in one of his sermons.

Wealthy and teeming with vice, Carthage burned with
eroticism. Some men impassioned by art, others with drink,
lived among flowers and sweet smells. There was hardly a
street or a square in the city that did not conceal a brothel.
The citizens vaunted lewdness and lived under the sign of
the goddess Tanit.

Augustine wrote later: "We assisted with great attention
at the 'games' everywhere going on beneath our eyes among
the followers of the virgin goddess Tanit. Shameful rites
were carried on among them and all manner of obscenities.
It was well known what was pleasing to this 'virginal' goddess.

"As for the cult of the *Magna Mater*, historians said that
it gave utterance to the songs of nature, but if so, this was
in a way shameful for them to be heard not by the mother
of the gods but by any honest citizen."

When Romanianus came to Carthage he included his
young protégé in his costly pleasures. In the voluptuous city
Carthago Veneris (Carthage of Venus) Augustine found real
enchantment of the senses.

The city was grandiose in its size.² From the steps of the
temple of Asculapius on the summit of the Acropolis spread
out an unforgettable view of the best planned of the world's
capitals and its two oval ports. This was the Carthage of
which Vergil sang, rich in history and legend, more the mistress of the sea than Rome was because it was closer to it.

Augustine eagerly mixed with the crowds in the public
squares and on the streets. He expected everything from this
most enchanting of pagan cities. He was in love with love,
and hungered for it.

As all Mediterranean men, the young student delighted in
the amusements held everywhere in Carthage: chariot races,
gladiatorial combats, tragedies and comedies, operas and bal-
lets. He laughed and wept at the comedies of Terence and
the gentle Menander.

"Why is it that man likes to grieve over doleful and tragic

events which he would not want to happen to himself? The spectator likes to experience grief at such scenes, and this very sorrow is like a pleasure to him. What is this but a pitiable folly? For the more a man is moved by these things, the less free is he from such passions. . . . He will show greater approval of the author of such representations, the greater the grief he feels. But if men's misfortunes, whether fictitious or in ancient times, are put on in such manner that the spectator does not feel sorrow, then he leaves in disgust and with disapproval. If grief is aroused in him, he remains in the theater, full of attention and enjoying himself. . . . While no man wants to be wretched, does he nevertheless want to be merciful?"

The African Rome also revealed to Augustine the imposing grandeur of the Empire. One could take pride in belonging to the City, in one's status as a full-fledged Roman citizen, in having a share in the greatness, the glory and even the ancestral traditions of the Romans. Carthage was a veritable Babel, but a well-knit, coherent Babel, united in an exalted idea of the Empire. It was true it held a diversity of races, religions, and contradictory passions, but every man was first of all a Roman and, like all neophytes, gloried in it; he shared in the Roman order and in "the peace of Rome."

Augustine threw himself headlong into a life that was at once easygoing and studious. He was greedy, a glutton, and never satisfied. He joined, of course, a band of rowdies who annoyed the teachers and ragged the new students. They called themselves the "Wreckers." When their misdeeds became too serious, they were whipped and returned to their families. Augustine was one of their number, but he was careful not to go too far, for he wanted to continue with his studies.

Apuleius of Madaura wrote: "The first work is done by the teacher who begins to polish the roughness of the boy's mind. Then comes the grammarian who lays down a ground-

work in various subjects; finally it is the turn of the rhetorician who places in his hand the weapon of eloquence."

After the first teacher in Tagaste and the grammarian of
Madaura, Augustine was now ready for the rhetorician of
Carthage. To remain in Carthage and finish his promising
studies, he had again to call on the inexhaustible generosity
of Romanianus. Patricius had died suddenly, after becoming
a Christian, and Monica was not able to continue sending
her son the monthly allowance on which he depended.
Romanianus supplied this and, thanks to his benefactor, Augustine continued his life of hard study and dissipation.

He was an excellent student and the outstanding scholar
in his school. With furious energy he attacked the subjects
of rhetoric, dialectic, geometry, music, mathematics and also
a bit of Roman law—the last because his mother dreamed
of his becoming a lawyer or a politician. She wrote him
constantly, through the intermediary of the slave pedagogue,
stressing the advantage of this choice. He was to become an
accomplished rhetorician—*vir eloquentissimus*.

The rhetorician's profession could be either that of a
teacher or an advocate. Its rules were very rigorous, and were
classified, divided and subdivided, theory and practice being set by age-old tradition. The student must practice *dec-
lamation*, either persuasive (*suasona*) or juridical (con-
troversial). He had to learn *arrangement*, the art of com-
posing a discourse divided into six parts. There were fixed
rules for the *exorde* (to arouse sympathy, interest, attention);
for the *narration* (artfully interwoven into the discourse); for
elocution (correct expression, rhythm and ornaments of
style), etc.

A day marked with a red letter by Augustine was the one
when he discovered the later writings of Cicero and of Aulus
Gellius, "a man of great eloquence and vast and abundant
knowledge." In fact, Cicero's *Hortensius* became the starting
point of his future self-development.

"I studied the treatises on eloquence, in which I desired

to shine, for a damnable and inflated purpose, directed toward empty human joys. In the ordinary course of study I came upon a book by a certain Cicero, whose tongue almost all men admire, but not his heart. This work contains his exhortation to philosophy and is called *Hortensius*. This book changed my affections. It . . . caused me to have different purposes and desires. All my vain hopes forthwith became worthless to me, and with incredible ardor of heart I desired undying wisdom."

Up to the time of reading this work of Cicero (which has since been lost), Augustine had hesitated regarding the choice of a career. Now suddenly he decided: he would not become a lawyer but a teacher. He wanted to know and teach, to possess true *wisdom* as Cicero defined it.

But this, unfortunately, was not easy. It was along the uneasy and often precipitous paths of philosophy, or rather of philosophers, that Augustine would attain to Faith—much later.

It was during this first stay in Carthage that Augustine fell in with Manichaeans. He was to remain faithful to their doctrine for almost nine years.

Since he had been old enough to ask questions he had tried to "comprehend." What was the reason for life, death, virtue, pleasure or sorrow? What was the meaning of life? Everywhere he was met by a silence to him more deadly than the most terrifying of answers. The simple faith of his mother, the "apparent contradictions of the Scriptures" (the horrible happenings recorded in the Bible repelled him), satisfied him no more than the mediocre gods with whom his father had earlier been content.

He tried to read the Scriptures but met with disappointment. "None such as I was at that time could enter into it, nor could I bend my neck for its passageways." He preferred the clarity and logic of Cicero, Plato's disciple, without apocalypses, genealogies or symbols.

It was then he listened to the conversation of the Manichaeans who were among his fellow students. Manichaeism appealed to him in that it was not conformist. Manichaeans and pagans were not in public favor, for the Christian religion was the only official one and the imperial government condemned, although if it did not yet track down, the Perfect Ones. A State religion was necessary to Rome even if it changed that religion from time to time. This in itself was a reason for young people to become excited at contact with noncomformist doctrines.

"O Truth, Truth, how intimately did even the very marrow of my mind sigh for you." Perhaps the Manichaeans could calm his inquietude regarding the great problems of life and belief. In any case they had an answer to the anguishing questions: Whence is Evil? Why do men suffer misfortune and pain?

"I did not know that evil is only the privation of a good, even to the point of complete nonentity. . . . I did not know that true interior justice, which judges not according to custom but by the most righteous law of Almighty God."

It seemed to Augustine that the Christian doctrine put faith above all else, before reason and comprehension. Augustine's critical and contentious mind could not accept an implicit faith. On the other hand the dualistic explanation of the world, expounded by Mani,[3] satisfied him: The universe is divided into two domains—the kingdom of Light which is Good, that of Darkness which is Evil. The earth is the domain of Evil. Good and Evil have existed from all eternity, and the earth is the result of a mixture of good and bad elements; without the first there would be no good; without the second, no evil. (Did not St. Matthew say: A good tree cannot bring forth bad fruit?) Thus one was Light, the other Darkness, and they were at constant war, winning and losing alternately.

The Prince of Evil, or Matter, desired to conquer the kingdom of Light, and God sent forth Primal Man to fight

Satan. (Earthly life existed only because the devil had be-
got demons—even vegetation is in conflict with the elements
striving for liberation.) If all men had done their duty, Evil
would quickly have disappeared from the earth; since they
did not, it was desirable for the world to come to an end, and
Evil would dissolve with Matter.

Only the Elect, the disciples of the Paraclete, could succeed in escaping Evil. An Elect must leave his family and
give up everything he possessed. He must be poor and
humble, exemplary in his chastity. He must not even gather
the fruits of his garden and must prefer to die of hunger
rather than to take life of any kind. He must live on the fruit
and vegetables others give him in order to receive into his
miserable body the divine substance retained in those
plants. His meals must be accompanied by hymns and
prayers.

The conclusion of the Manichaean doctrine is that man's
unhappiness arises from his ties to matter, namely Evil. Since
life is an indecisive and deplorable struggle between God and
the Devil, the increase of the human race must be halted as
soon as possible. The chastity of the Elect had no other object than the end of mankind. The world would disappear in
an immense conflagration, from which only the souls of the
just would emerge living and purified.

All his life Augustine sought the explanation of Evil. Later
as a Doctor of the Church, he devoted many pages of his
writings to the thesis that it was caused by man's sinfulness.
He even demonstrated that sorrow and pain can be for men
an element of moral progress.

But in Carthage, at eighteen years of age, Evil and pain
were incomprehensible to him. The Manichaeans suggested
an explanation—he accepted it.

Moreover, the Manichaeans did not require him to sacrifice his pleasures (in particular the pleasures of the flesh) in
which he set such store. He would never be an Elect, but
only a Hearer, a "sympathizer" as we say today, a lecturer

and an eloquent propagandist of the Manichaean teachings.
This is the reason that later he took so much trouble to
demolish a theology he had once accepted. To assuage his
own conscience he felt he must pull down, stone by stone,
the edifice of Manichaeism. Many times and with great
anxiety he returned to this question. This Christian philosopher and doctrinarian was essentially a tormented man and
would so remain until the day of his death. He always wrote
first to convince himself.

There were in Africa seventy-two Manichaean bishops and
twelve Masters who constituted a sort of directive body presided over by a supreme chief representing Mani. At the
same time there were the Hearers who followed rules much
less austere. If they fasted on Sunday, they could eat meat
on other days; they could possess goods and property. They
were permitted to marry and to have a sexual life, but must
try to avoid having children in order not to prolong the
Purgatory of earthly existence.[4] Because of the good will they
showed, these Hearers could qualify, in a later life, to be re-
born in the perfection of the Elect.

Augustine was eager for life, and wanted its every experience. Although he was drawn to Manichaeism, he could
not decide to make the renunciations required to become an
Elect, and was to content himself with being a Hearer. He
had a great admiration for the Perfect who made these renunciations, but he did not have the strength to imitate them.
Carthage offered him every manner of pleasure and he had
not tired of it.

Even so, he flung himself with all his native energy into
his new faith. He took part in the assemblies, facing the
Sun; he received the imposition of hands by the Elect; he
assisted fervently at the feast of Bema on the anniversary
of Mani's crucifixion.

He took part in debates in which the Christians were attacked. In these he unleashed a furious eloquence and was
often victorious, for he revealed himself a formidable master

of dialectic, a persuasive orator, convincing and irresistible despite his harsh voice, which was often hoarse and breathless from asthma. His preaching of the principles of the dualistic dogma made many converts, and he gloried in his success, for there was nothing more heady than influence over other men.

"If I permitted myself to be dragged along, it was because they claimed to lead their hearers to God and deliver them from error by the use of pure reason." The last word is the one to be stressed—Augustine had need of *reason*. The dualistic explanation seemed sufficient: God did not wish Evil, but he permitted it; He fought against it and would one day triumph. He was not yet All Powerful since Evil existed, but when the experiment of life had ended, then Evil would be conquered and God would shine forth in all his splendor—the One and All.

During those years Africa was seething beneath the abuses and extortions of Romanius, the Roman governor. The provincial delegates carried their grievances to the Emperor Valentinian, but Romanius had strong supporters at the imperial court. Despite proofs of his guilt, he retained his post.

Now in 372, just as Augustine arrived in Carthage, a prince of the federated Moors, Firmus by name, led a revolt against Romanius and, proclaiming himself the "Emperor of Africa," assumed the purple. Almost without striking a blow, he seized the larger part of Mauretania. Those places where he did meet with resistance he pillaged and destroyed; thus Caesarea (Algeria) was put to the torch. The Donatist schismatics (against whom an imperial decree had recently been promulgated), seeing this secession as an unexpected African victory, rallied to Firmus against Rome.

The Donatist schism was specifically African and was not in its beginnings, to speak properly, a schism at all. It

stemmed from a dispute that arose at the time of the consecration of Caecilian, the bishop of Carthage, in 311.

To quote Ernest Stein in his *Histoire du Bas Empire:*

"When Maxentius put an end to the persecution of the
Christians in 307, Caecilian had been archdeacon of the
Carthaginian Church; but Felix, the bishop who consecrated
him, was accused of having handed over to the Roman authorities during the persecution the Sacred Books and altar
vessels, and thus of being an apostate and a traitor (*traditor*).

"Immediately a synod of seventy African bishops, hostile
to Caecilian, declared Felix unworthy of the episcopal office
and for this reason annulled Caecilian's consecration and
proceeded to elect in his place Majorinus, another member
of the clergy of Carthage. This was not accepted by Caecilian
and his followers, and the Church of Africa was split into
two violently opposing factions.

"When the Emperor Constantine sent Caecilian a sum of
money to be used for the Catholics of Africa he thus recognized his claim as head of the official church, and Majorinus' partisans protested, calling for the Emperor's arbitra-
tion of the dispute. Constantine replied by convoking a synod
composed of Gaulish and Italian bishops.

"This synod met at Rome, October 2, 313. Majorinus had
died, and the priest Donatus had succeeded him. This is the
reason the sect assumed the name 'Donatist.' The synod in
Rome decided in favor of Caecilian, but the Donatists refused to accept the verdict. The Emperor then assembled at
Arles, on August 1, 314, a new council of thirty-three bishops
to re-examine the case. Again Caecilian was upheld, and the
inquiry proved that Felix had not been a *traditor*. Most of
the Donatists refused to accept these decisions.

"In 315 Constantine promulgated the sentence unfavor-
able to the Donatists and ordered the suppression of the
schism. From 316 on, a state of complete anarchy prevailed
in Africa. In 320, it appeared that real *traditores* were to be

found among the Donatist bishops; nevertheless, they were accorded toleration until 347.

"In this year Constantius, son and successor to Constantine the Great, decided to put an end to the Donatists. The churches were taken from the sect; their religious services were forbidden; their clergy were exiled. Donatus himself died at sea as he was being deported.

"The schismatics thereupon allied themselves with nationalistic bandits who were terrorizing the country and were known as *Circumcellions*. Thus supported by elements inimical to Rome, Donatism took on a character hostile not only to the Empire but to the official Church of Africa.

"When the pagan Emperor Julian came into power he reinstated the Donatist bishops, a measure which led to bloody uprisings. Julian assembled at Constantinople, during the winter of 362, the leaders of the various confessions, avowedly to bring them to agreement, but in reality to turn their bitter dissentions against Christianity itself. The principal divergence in doctrine (because there had to be one, after all) came from the fact that the Donatists insisted on the rebaptism of Christians who had originally been baptized by 'unworthy' priests. The Catholic Church considers that baptism is valid as a sacrament no matter what the moral quality of the one who administers it, a theological point of view which it has ever maintained.

"In February 373, Valentinian forbade the Donatists to rebaptize, and as a result they turned their allegiance to Firmus, who led the revolt of the Moorish tribes against Rome.

"Firmus immediately declared Donatism to be the religion of his State, and rallied to his 'throne' the Circumcellions, allowing them to take vengeance on the Catholics."

Everywhere there were massacres, crimes, night attacks on women and solitary individuals, personal vengeances. The Circumcellions demanded contributions from everyone, assassinated those who resisted and even those who paid. Rome's reaction was very weak—would she let the situation degenerate and risk, by default, the loss of Africa?

Finally, in 375, the central government decided to take action and sent to Africa the able general Theodosius who had earlier distinguished himself in Britain in the campaign against the Alemanni. Brave and patriotic and firmly determined to put down the rebellion once for all, he fought his way to the walls of Tipasa. There in the last stronghold of the revolt, his assault was successful and Firmus committed suicide.

Now the African people brought before Theodosius their earlier complaints against Romanius. Point by point, the governor defended himself, but the general was soon convinced of his guilt and decided to arrest him and send him to Rome for trial. It is possible that Theodosius himself had some ambitions for personal power, but what follows is a dark story of political villainy.

In Rome, Romanius defended himself fiercely, even to the point of bringing down on his head the threats of Merobaudius, a powerful Germanic general in Rome and a commander of the militia. However, in the end the Emperor Valentinian decided not to condemn Romanius. This victory was not enough for the African governor, and at once he turned his venom against Theodosius, the author of his downfall. As a result of his intrigues, General Theodosius was accused of plotting against the State and, arrested in Carthage, was condemned and beheaded.

(A short time afterward Valentinian nonetheless commanded the services of Theodosius' son, the future emperor of the East, to conquer the Sarmatians and Suevi on the banks of the Rhine.)

When Valentinian I died of apoplexy in 375, two Caesars were elected: Valerius in the East and Gratian. It was then decided, in order quickly to stem the ambitions of the barbarian general Merobaudius, to raise Valentinian's son to the purple. Flavius Valentinian II was only four years of age and was immediately placed under the tutelage of Gratian, now promoted to the rank of first Augustus.

During young Valentinian's childhood, a preponderant influence at court was that of the Bordeaux poet and philosopher Ausonius. It was due to him that the reign began as "intellectual" and liberal; an almost general amnesty was proclaimed and measures were taken for the protection of citizens.

At this period the Popes were endeavoring to establish their jurisdiction and to give it precise status. The bishops, who up to that time had been jealous of their independence, gradually accustomed themselves to seek the advice of Rome (on questions of canon law, particularly). Pope Siricius, for example, fixed the minimum age of deacons at thirty years, of priests at thirty-three, and at forty-five for bishops. He definitely forbade marriage for the clergy of all the major orders.[5]

Thus were sown the seeds of the divorce between the two Churches of Rome and Byzantium, a consequence of the separation of the two Empires.

Chapter Three

YOUNG MANHOOD
374–383

Now Augustine was to know love. Since coming to Carthage
he had thrown himself headlong into adventures of all kinds
with all the tempestuousness of his demanding nature.

"In my joy I was bound about with painful chains of iron,
so that I might be scourged by burning rods of jealousy, and
suspicion, and fear, and anger, and quarreling."

These were the feverish passions of a student, always present yet without deep influence on the course of his studies.
But this time he was truly and sincerely in love with one
who was to be his companion for many years. Louis Bertrand
calls her "Modesta," but there is no other source for this,
and Augustine never names her in his writings.

Who was she exactly? No one will ever know. She was a
girl he met in Carthage, of very modest extraction, probably
the daughter of a manumitted slave. What she was doing in
Carthage or how she lived there, we cannot answer, for St.
Augustine carefully hid all traces. Perhaps the whole affair
started with one of his numerous nightly adventures or during some hour of amusement. Great loves are sometimes
born in such a way.

From one day to the other, Augustine ceased his wandering life. He rented a small house on the slopes of the
Acropolis, and there the young couple made their home.

As Romanianus' liberality did not extend to the upkeep of a household, Augustine was obliged to give lessons at the same time that he pursued his studies.

"In those years I taught the art of rhetoric, and being vanquished by greed, I sold a skill at speech designed for victories at court. I preferred . . . to have good students—such, that is, as are called good—and without deceit I taught them to be deceitful. . . .

"In those years I had a woman companion, not one joined to me in what is named lawful wedlock, but one whom my wandering passion, empty of prudence, had picked up. But I had this one only, and moreover I was faithful to her bed. With her I learned at first hand how great a distance lies between the restraint of a conjugal covenant, mutually made for the sake of begetting offspring, and the bargain of a lustful love, where a child is born against our will, although once born he forces himself upon our love."

This last was true. Augustine soon became the father of a little boy, Adeodatus. Suddenly, several months later and without anyone knowing why, Augustine made ready to leave Carthage and come back to Tagaste. Perhaps he had won his diplomas, but the return to Tagaste raised many problems. He nevertheless resolved to go, for was he not making his living in the African capital where rhetoricians and teachers were far more plentiful than in Tagaste?

Perhaps, too, his reputation as a Manichaean was beginning to weigh against him with the parents of his pupils in Carthage. In any event, he decided to return with his "concubine" and little Adeodatus. He was not, however, received back in the manner of the Prodigal Son. Monica had learned of his "turpitudes" and could not decide whether to lament more his Manichaeism or his outrageous liaison. She wept more bitterly "than mothers weep over their children's dead bodies."

When Augustine wrote her to prepare her for his return to Tagaste, she refused to receive him under her roof. She went further. Despite her sorrow—for she adored her son—she decided not even to see this Manichaean and adulterer. She would henceforth devote herself to her other two children; she would disown Augustine. Yet at the bottom of her heart she knew he was her favorite. It was she who had first divined his great talents, and now she knew only fear as to how he would use them.

The good Romanianus, who had become a Manichaean under Augustine's influence, welcomed his protégé with open arms. He would arrange here and there for him to give lessons in grammar, in which Augustine excelled. These lessons would insure his material existence, and Romanianus also would have him open the doors of rhetoric to his own son, Licentius.

Once back in Tagaste, Augustine soon wielded surprising authority. It doubtless was easy for him to dominate his fellow townsmen. He eloquently spread the Manichaean faith and quickly became the idol of a youthful circle who accepted him as their model. He lost no time in converting many of Romanianus' friends and his own comrades, among them his friend Alypius and Romanianus' son, Licentius.

Under Romanianus' wing, life was luxurious. Augustine immersed himself in easy living and the enjoyment of satisfied vanity. He was brilliant, supremely intelligent, admired.

All this while Monica died a thousand deaths. She thought perhaps Augustine would disregard her interdict and try to see her. He did nothing of the sort. One night she had the following dream: She saw herself standing weeping on a "wooden rule" and coming toward her a young man "splendid, joyful, and smiling upon her." When she explained the cause of her grief, he told her to rest secure and bade her look about her and she would see that "where she was," there her son was also. And when she looked, she saw Augustine standing on the same rule.

The following day she arranged to meet Augustine on one of the streets of Tagaste. The interview between them was both tender and bitter, and Monica was on the verge of tears. She mastered herself, however, and succeeded in telling her son about her dream. Then breaking down, she implored him to cast off all his errors and return to the family roof.

Augustine did not seem troubled and immediately sought cleverly to "interpret" his mother's dream. He came up with the answer that the dream meant Monica would become a Manichaean. It was quite obvious!

Monica violently rejected this explanation. "No!" she cried. "He said, 'Where you are, there also is he.' I am a Christian."

Without replying, Augustine turned his back on her, and disappeared into the crowded street.

Around the same time he lost his best friend, a young man, "my equal in age, flowering like me with youth, and very dear to me because of community of interests." They had grown up together, had been at the same school, and had played games together. Augustine had led him away from his faith and "toward those superstitions and pernicious fables because of which my mother wept over me."

This young man had been stricken by fever and lay for a long time unconscious. He was hastily baptized while in this state, and after several hours he revived and regained his senses. As soon as he could talk, Augustine, who had not left him all the while, tried to joke with him about "that baptism which he had received when he was far away in mind and sense," and vigorously denounced the measure taken under such circumstances. To the great surprise of the apostle of Manichaeism, "he was horrified at me as if I were an enemy." The baptism he had received even while unconscious seemed to have affected the young man profoundly. Augustine decided to wait until his friend was well to renew his attack. But after a few days the fever struck again and his poor friend died.

Augustine was overcome with sorrow and "whatever I looked upon was death." His native place was "a torment to me," and in his unhappy state everything about him was a source of irritation and torture. He was sick, he had become "a great riddle" to himself. He marveled that other men lived when he whom he loved was dead. Burying himself in his affliction, he raged and wept. He could find no peace, no reason for anything, and it seemed to him he had entered a dark and endless tunnel.

He did not know what to do to regain his balance and to get away from his thoughts. There was only one road open: he must quickly flee from the familiar places where "half of his soul" had lived and where everything had become a horror to him, even the very light itself.

Distraught and half mad, Augustine decided to leave Tagaste. But where would he go? The best solution would surely be to return to Carthage where he could lose himself in its noisy, engrossing, restless life. There he could find work.

Through a third person Monica learned of her son's sudden flight, for he left without seeing her. She went for advice to the bishop of Tagaste and besought him to bring Augustine back to the ways of faith and reason. Was he not on the road to perdition and what would become of him?

The bishop gently refused, saying, "Let him be. Only pray to the Lord in his behalf. He will find out by reading what is the character of that error and how great is its impiety."

Monica's tears continued to flow at her son's condition and her own.

"Go away from me now," the bishop then said. "It is impossible that the son of such tears should perish."

Augustine was to spend eight years in Carthage (from 375 to 383). There he taught rhetoric and was joined by Alypius, a boyhood friend, who was studying law and was to become a Roman magistrate.

Life was difficult, for there were too many teachers, and the students were hard to control. In addition little Adeodatus was always hungry, and Modesta had to perform miracles to keep up their small household and to make both ends meet.

Augustine, at grips with material difficulties which embittered him and dampened his spirits, nevertheless struggled on—Romanianus' generosity was not, after all, inexhaustible. He taught rhetoric and even grammar whenever he could, and started to write. He had always had a great love for poetry, and he wrote verses which he recited in public in the Roman manner. He proved himself an excellent reader, even actor, and was often admired and applauded. At those times when his purse was thin, what could have been more consoling? He was happier and had a handful of disciples who followed him blindly. As Alypius and Licentius were soon joined by Nebridius, Fortunatus and others, he was soon the head of a clan if not of a school.

But within himself he was not satisfied despite this flattery to his vanity. An impetuous son always reacts against the demands of a possessive mother. Doubtless he had become a Manichaean largely as a gesture against Monica. But he knew regret, even remorse.

Moreover, he was becoming convinced that the truth, the absolute he so ardently wished to know could not be found in the teachings of Mani. When he asked for explanations, the Perfect Ones avoided giving an answer.

"I believed that evil is some such (corporal) substance and that it possesses its own foul and hideous mass, either gross, which the Manichaeans styled the earth, or thin and subtle, as is the air, which they imagine to be a malignant mind stealing through the earth. . . . I postulated two masses opposed to one another, each of them infinite, but the evil one on a narrower scale, the good one larger. From this pestilential beginning other blasphemies pursued me. . . .

"I thought myself to be more truly religious if I believed You to be infinite in other parts even though I was forced to admit that You are finite in that part where the evil mass stands in opposition to You, than if I thought that in all

Your parts You were bounded by the form of the human body. . . . Our Savior himself, Your Only-begotten Son, I so thought of as being something extruded out of the mass of Your pellucid substance for our salvation. I could believe nothing of Him except what I could picture by my own vain powers. I judged that such a nature as His could never be born of the Virgin Mary without becoming intermingled in the flesh. How such a thing as I had figured out for myself could be thus intermingled and yet undefiled I could not see."

Since the Manichaeans could not answer his questions, Augustine had to search out other sources, other roads to truth. He became interested in the astrologers who claimed there was in the heavens a *cause* which, despite ourselves, throws us into sin. Either Venus, Mars, or Saturn lead us to such and such an action—a theory which tends to exonerate men and place all blame on Fate, and which was not incompatible with the Manichaean ideas. Man's inability to escape his destiny led to resignation, and was, from certain points of view, a doctrine offering consolation. There was nothing very inspiring about it except that the seeker's curiosity kept him on the quest.

A contest in dramatic poetry was held in Carthage around that time, and Augustine won the first prize. Vindicianus, who placed the crown on his head, was proconsul of Carthage, and a highly skilled physician. He interested himself in Augustine personally and the young man confided to him that he belonged to the Manichaean sect as a Hearer, and was an active practitioner of astrology.

The old proconsul answered that he himself had been interested in astrology in other days, but he had given it up. He tried to dissuade Augustine from going on with studies which he considered sterile and false, even deceptive and dangerous.

Another friend, Firminus by name, told Augustine he had learned from his father that he, Firminus, was born on the same day and at the identical hour as the son of the servant of one of his father's friends. They grew up side by side, but Firminus, born under the same stars, had risen through his own efforts to high places, whereas the slave had remained in the same miserable condition into which he was born. Although Augustine had some reservations to make as to the matter being so simple as all that, Firminus' story nevertheless gave him food for thought.

Augustine was also intrigued by the predictions and writings of Albicerius, the soothsayer. Mystery, the inexplicable, lured him irresistibly and he saturated himself in what he could learn of supernatural phenomena, the *abyssus humanae*.

Slowly he advanced on the road to success. New disciples came to hear him teach, among them Horatius, Marcianus and Eulogius. All became Manichaeans, so great were his powers of persuasion.

Toward the year 380, when he was twenty-six years of age, he wrote his first book, *On the Beautiful and the Fitting*. He dedicated it to Hierius, one of the orators of Rome who was then in great vogue. Augustine had never met Hierius, but the latter's reputation was tremendous and the young poet admired and envied him. "Orator of the City of Rome"—what career could be more glorious!

On the Beautiful and the Fitting was a book in which the Manichaean doctrine and the influence of Cicero were mixed but did not fuse. Probably only a very small number of copies of the manuscript were made, and in any case these soon disappeared. (We do not doubt that Augustine had a hand in this matter.)

The following would seem to have been the theme of this treatise on aesthetics: A thing is pleasing in itself—this we call beauty; but the fact that it pleases arises from its relationship to something other—this we call fittingness. He had read Aristotle's *Categories* and immediately began to teach them, for he had immersed himself in their study.

His book received little notice. We do not even know if

Hierius acknowledged its receipt to his young African colleague.

As time passed, life weighed Augustine down more and
more. The students were unbearable, and the disorders that
took place among them were "a shameful thing." No one
was safe from their insults and Augustine with his weak voice,
and often lost in his own thoughts, was ragged more often
than the other teachers.

He wanted to push on with his own research, but books
were rare in Carthage, and only a few persons around him
could discuss them intelligently with him. He was easily the
victor in any philosophical or religious discussion in which
he engaged. The rest of the time he was beating his fist
vainly against hollow walls.

Then in his quest for truth, he began to have doubts regarding the foundations of the Manichaean doctrine. He had
met only mediocre priests, second-rate members of the Elect.
He needed to listen to the heads of the Order, ask them
questions, penetrate to the core of the essential beliefs concerning Good and Evil.

At last came the time when he was able to meet one of the
great lights among the Manichaeans. Faustus, the bishop of
Milevis in Numidia, came to Carthage and Augustine
looked forward with delight to the training he would receive
and the discussions he would have with this higher member
of the Elect.

At first Augustine found Faustus gracious and pleasant,
and that "on the topics on which they usually speak he
could talk along more agreeably than the others." Augustine
asked questions and insisted when Faustus failed to reply.
He wanted to know, to understand, he was waiting for the
light. But Faustus amiably refused to engage in discussion.

"I was concerned not with what vessel of discourse but
with what knowledge this Faustus, so renowned among
them, would put before me to eat."

Now Faustus was a pleasing speaker, sometimes even

eloquent. On the other hand, he was a mediocre grammarian and his knowledge of philosophy was poor. Unlike Augustine, he had not read the Scriptures and had no competence in astronomy (although the Manichaeans claimed to be able to explain, according to the Eastern tradition, the course of the stars through the heavens).

Augustine lost hope that Faustus could solve the problems that perplexed him. The man was very modest in his manner, and knowing he understood little about what was asked him, he did not wish to engage in disputation since it would scarcely turn out to his advantage; his adversary was much too strong. Augustine was greatly disappointed. His enthusiasm was dampened when he saw how poorly equipped was this great doctor of the Manichaeans.

At this time the government was tightening its net around the Manichaeans, who had come under the interdict of Theodosius. Some were arrested and even tortured; others went into hiding among small clandestine groups of their coreligionists. Augustine did not feel ready to die for a cause which had disappointed him, and he no longer felt safe in Carthage.

Moreover, strange rumors were abroad of the "exemplary" life of some of the Elect. One Elect had made a girl pregnant and one day on a public square "three of the Elect took drink and behaved in so obscene a manner as to surpass the licentiousness of the grossest of men."

Augustine also knew that he could do nothing more to advance his career in Carthage. The time had come for a change, to seek elsewhere the food for his ambition. Rome was his objective and he would try his fortunes there.

From Faustus he obtained a warm recommendation to his colleague, the Manichaean bishop of Rome. A personal friend would lodge him temporarily in the "African quarter."

Augustine hastened the plans for his voyage, one might almost say his flight. Monica, anxious on hearing the threats being made against the Manichaeans, came in haste to Carthage to urge her son to renounce this heresy and to return to Tagaste. Augustine knew he could not tell his mother of his intended departure for Italy and decided he would leave secretly in order to escape her. She was suspicious and would not leave her son's side. Augustine therefore played a trick on her. One day he declared he was going to accompany a friend to the port, and left his home just as night was falling. Monica followed him to the shore where the vessel was waiting, but its departure was delayed because there was no wind to push it into the channel. Augustine said he would wait until the last moment to bid his friend farewell.

In the end Monica fell asleep on the steps of the oratory dedicated to St. Cyprian, the patron of Carthage. The wind rose at daybreak, and the ship left the African coast with Augustine on it, while Monica peacefully slept on.

"She loved me to be present with her, after the custom of mothers, but much more than many mothers. . . . With groans she besought what she had brought forth with groans."

When she awakened, Monica abandoned herself to her grief. She lamented bitterly, reproaching her son for his hardness of heart and his deceit. Then she "went home, and I went on to Rome," where Modesta and Adeodatus would rejoin him when he had found lodgings and work.

Chapter Four

FROM ROME TO MILAN
383–385

The young Roman citizen was in the grip of great emotion as he approached his spiritual fatherland, for although Augustine was African in race and heart, his cast of mind and his education were Roman. From Ostia to Rome, as each step brought him closer to the Eternal City, he was filled with understandable joy. He was soon to walk those famous streets trod by Vergil hundreds of years before—Vergil, the poet of his predilection—and by Cicero who had instilled in him the taste for wisdom.

He knew one great city, Carthage, but Rome was more marvelous still. He would see the Capitol; he would loiter in the Forum; would attend the circus games in the real Colosseum.

The Forum was that vast esplanade surrounded by a portico, supported on the entrance side (the south) by a simple row of columns, on the other three sides by a double colonnade. On the eastern end, against the marble wall in the curved form of a hemicycle, rose the equestrian statue of Augustus, the first emperor, in gilded bronze. Between the peripheral columns were statues of famous men who either by word or sword had served the Empire well. Ascending three marble steps, one reached the entrance of the Ulpian basilica, surpassing even the Forum in magnificence and surrounded by a portico with niches also filled with statues. Beyond this rose the two rectangular libraries of Ulpia, one devoted to books in Greek, the other to Latin literature and the imperial archives. Between the two libraries was a quadrangle with Trajan's Column in the center.

And there was the admirable Forum of Trajan where the masters of literature gathered their students and propounded their teachings as in the days of Marcus Aurelius. Above the majestic brick hemicycle mounted five stories containing a hundred and fifty market shops. On the ground floor, on the Forum level, fruit and flowers were sold; on the second floor were the shops of sellers of wine and oil; on the third and fourth, were found rare produce and spices from the East. Finally, on top, were the tanks of the sellers of fish, supplied by pipes carrying in seawater from Ostia.

Augustine saw too for the first time the splendor of the Quirinal Palace, before which the Emperor Constantius had cried out in delight when he made his entry into Rome in 356.

When Augustine arrived in Rome, the capital counted 1,200,000 inhabitants. It contained around three thousand palaces and opulent dwellings and some sixty thousand habitations, several stories high, into which were crowded the miserable plebeians. Nowhere else did the differences of lot seem so complete, so cruel, as in Rome. On one hand, the poor and the slaves; on the other, persons with vast fortunes, drawing revenues up to two million in gold a year. The wealthy led an indolent life in their splendid palaces where constant feasting and entertainments were held. (Gold was used even for the harnesses of their mules.)

It was not in one of the palaces that our poor little professor of rhetoric was to be installed, but in one of the miserable *insulae* of five or six stories, where the people were housed under unbelievably crowded conditions and without comforts of any kind. There, free workmen or slave domestics lived, cooked, ate and slept in complete promiscuity.

Viewed from outside, these colossal *insulae*, or moderate-rent dwellings, were alike in their ugliness and cheap construction. The street façades were dreary and lifeless, and in each a stone staircase led from the ground level to a landing where a ladder was used to reach the higher stories. The landlord, to compel delinquent payments of rent, had generally only to remove the ladder leading up to the tenant's lodging. These houses of brick and wood burned down frequently, for the risk of fire was great in a place where portable stoves had to be depended on for heating, and candles and torches for light.

As with all Romans, even the wealthy, the furniture consisted mainly of beds. One slept on these beds at night, sat on them to eat and receive guests, to read and write in the daytime. Here among the poor, the beds were masonry bunks attached to the walls and covered with mattresses of straw.

In most of these workmen's houses the windows were not even covered by sheets of mica. Those within were protected against cold and rain by hangings of cloth or skins, often beaten by the wind or saturated by the downpour, or else by wooden shutters with one or two ventilation holes which did not keep out the rain, the cold, or the winds, but at the same time excluded any light. Heating conditions were even worse. There were no chimneys in the *insulae*, neither was there running water. The water in Rome came from the mountains and was dispensed by a number of fountains, but it was not distributed to the poorer quarters.

The rents of these slum dwellings were high. Most of the houses were rented by their owners to agents, who sublet them "furnished" at usury rates. There were no public laws or regulations to prevent such practices.

Although the emperor and the court had left Rome for Milan, in all eyes Rome remained as the capital, visited by the greatest number of Roman or barbarian travelers. Despite economic crises, becoming more frequent, the city's population was constantly growing.

The political situation (in the city of Rome particularly) was also disturbing. The Emperor Gratian had taken coercive measures against pagans and their worship. But the prefect of Rome, the poet and philosopher Symmachus, was a staunch pagan as were most of the rich men and the intellectuals of the city. Gratian had abolished the tax immunity of the pagan colleges of pontiffs, had confiscated their inherited revenues, and removed the statue and altar of Victory from the assembly hall of the Senate.

The stubborn opposition—sometimes open, sometimes veiled—met by Gratian showed how great was the revival of pagan strength in Rome since Julian had given encouragement to the religion of the gods. A delegation of Roman senators journeyed to the court in Milan to persuade Gratian to revoke his edict. The Christian senators, supported by Pope Damasus and Ambrose, the bishop of Milan, convinced the emperor that he should refuse to receive the delegation. This ostracism only served to increase the religious zeal of the pagan senators, among them Pretextatus, Nicomacus Flavian and especially Symmachus, who now proceeded to restore the ruined sanctuaries as best they could and to assume themselves the expenses of worship.

Then the relations of the emperor and the Pope suddenly deteriorated when Gratian restored to the followers of a Spanish schismatic, Priscillian, the churches from which they had been expelled.

In that year of 383, Magnus Maximus, a distant relative of Theodosius, had himself proclaimed emperor by the troops in Britain. Having assumed the purple, he crossed the Channel to combat Gratian on European soil. Gratian's army, sent out to meet the usurper, was destroyed near Paris and those who survived went over to the allegiance of Maximus.

Just as Augustine arrived in Rome, news was received of Gratian's assassination at Lyon on August 25. It was said that Justina, the widow of Valentinian I, had taken over power in Milan in the name of her son, Valentinian II, twelve years of age, who was thenceforth the first Augustus. At the same time Bauton, the master of the militia (and an avowed pagan), was defending the Alpine heights against Maximus, who set up his stronghold at Trier since he could not win entry into Italy. In Constantinople, Theodosius, Valerius' successor, proclaimed himself Valentinian's protector and threatened intervention.

Such was the condition of the Empire and of the city when Augustine arrived in Rome.

Augustine found lodgings in the "African quarter" with a Manichaean Hearer. Soon after his arrival, he fell grievously ill. Autumn is the time of mists and malaria, and Rome at this season was far from healthy. Stricken with fever, Augustine soon lay in danger of death.

"I was on the verge of going down to hell. . . . My fever grew worse within me. Where would I have gone, if I had then left this world. . . . Of all this my mother knew nothing, yet far away she continued to pray for me."

Despite his dangerous condition, he did not ask for baptism. He was still a Manichaean. No doubt with good care he would recover.

"You caused me to recover from that illness, and then also You healed the son of Your handmaid, for a time as to his body, so that he might live and You might give him a better and a more certain health."

As soon as he recovered, he set out in search of pupils. He had to knock at many doors to solicit these lessons, to walk the streets in the autumn rain which is so heavy in Rome, "wandering like an exile among the dark Roman palaces and along the muddy pavements."

He was a poor teacher of rhetoric, trying to earn a living. After going up and down stairs, climbing the ramps of the City of Seven Hills from the Aventine to the Janiculum, bruising his feet on the pebbles of alleyways, in danger of being crushed by the chariots, begging the favor of the slave *nomenclator* who might furnish suitable introductions, he returned exhausted each night to the Velabrian quarter, to a street known today as the Via Greca. This quarter swarmed with a wretched horde of Eastern peoples; Oriental immigrants, Greeks, Syrians, Armenians, laborers, carriers, and dock workers lived crowded together. How far away Romanianus' luxurious dwelling seemed to Augustine as he shivered before an ill-lit brazier in the dim flicker of a small clay lamp, in cold and solitude!

Augustine associated with the Manichaeans, not only with his friends among the Hearers, but also several of the Elect. He still believed that it is not ourselves who sin but a sort of "other nature" which is within us.

"It gave joy to my pride to be above all guilt, and when I did an evil deed, not to confess that I myself had done it, so that You might heal my soul, since it had sinned against You. I loved to excuse myself, and to accuse I knew not what other being that was present with me but yet was not I."

He lived with a Manichaean because, since they were persecuted, the faithful formed a sort of freemasonry among themselves. Moreover, they were protected by certain prominent pagans, for there existed between pagans and Manichaeans secret agreements for defense and mutual aid.

It was through a loyal Manichaean friend that Augustine was introduced into a circle of cultivated pagans, they too the objects of imperial persecutions. Since various decrees launched by the emperors after Julian's death had suppressed (theoretically) both Manichaeism and paganism, it was modish to be either a Manichaean or a pagan in opposition to the regime.

From his first encounter with these learned men, who were excellent dialecticians and Epicureans desiring to preserve the old Latin culture, and who swore either by the gods or by Cicero, Augustine's interest was held captive. Already Cicero had shown him the way to wisdom in *Hortensius*; he found Cicero's influence still lived in Rome. His enthusiasm grew,

for his loss of faith in Manichaeism early inclined him toward the skepticism of the "Academics." His taste for life's
delights (in particular his need for sensual pleasure) was
also responsible for his somewhat hesitant leaning toward
Epicurean ideas.

He loved to spend long evenings in discourse with these
subtle minds. At last he could debate with men whose intelligence was on a level with his own. Such subjects were discussed as the structure of the universe and its laws, such
questions asked as, "Is the soul immortal? If it is not, should
man place his happiness in sensual pleasure?" Or, "If the
soul dies with the body, does truth also die?" Or again,
"Should it be said that knowledge and truth are not the
same?"

Augustine soon came to believe that these men spoke as
the sages of old. However, their universe was limited to individual well-being, to material progress for the masses—they
were "radicals."

But where was the soul in all this? Augustine had never
completely forgotten the rudiments of the Christian faith
taught him by Monica in his early years. If he had violently
turned against her in becoming a Manichaean (doubtless
partly to escape from her), he had never questioned the
superiority of the spirit nor the immortality of the soul. The
skeptics doubted this, and what they said did not satisfy
Augustine. They interested and intrigued him, opening up
to him vistas of thought of which he had never dreamed
before.

We must remember the difficulties of education in those
days. To acquire and assimilate his vast knowledge, Augustine
had to make constant effort. Libraries were few and difficult
of access; the available books were not all that could be desired.

Fortunately he was soon joined in Rome by his friend
Alypius, the brother of his heart, who had been his pupil in
Carthage as well as his disciple in Tagaste. Although a Mani-

chaean (he was one of Augustine's converts), he already held a position in the imperial government, and was assessor to the imperial treasurer and had important connections. His was a practical mind, basically honest, and he was a great lover of the circus games.

Through his relationship, Augustus was able to find pupils and to hold classes in various houses. Little by little, the number of his students increased but he had trouble with them. They were not riotous as in Carthage, insolently invading a classroom and wrecking everything they found. But often a group would suddenly leave one teacher to study with another, counting it as nothing to be "false to their own word." Thus suddenly abandoned by a number of his pupils, Augustine was no less disgusted than he had been with the behavior of those in Carthage.

Abandonment by these students meant that Augustine was also without money. He held this against them. "In truth such men are vile in character; they fornicate against You out of love for passing, temporary trifles and filthy lucre, which defiles the hand that seizes it." He was holding the devil by the tail, and could not make up his mind whether or not he would send for Modesta and Adeodatus.

He consoled himself by going frequently with Alypius to the circus games at the Colosseum. He shared his enthusiasm for the fights between gladiators, whereas in Carthage such spectacles had disgusted him. When first dragged to the games, Alypius had sworn he would close his eyes during the combat. When they arrived and got whatever seats they could, the whole place was in a frenzy of savage delight. He closed his eyes, and when a man fell in the combat, he heard a mighty roar from the crowd. It struck him with such force that he was overcome by curiosity and opened his eyes. At this he was deeply stricken in the soul, and "drank in savagery." He fixed his eyes on the spectacle and took delight in the struggle, becoming drunk "on blood and pleasure." He became one with the crowd he had joined. He looked, he shouted, and bore away with him "a madness that would arouse him to return."

Augustine found great support in the friendship of Alypius whose scrupulous honesty and disinterestedness was admired by all his colleagues, although he himself could not see how he could act otherwise. His integrity had recently been put to a severe test. He was serving, as we know, in Rome as assessor to the imperial treasurer. A certain powerful senator, to whom many were bound by favors received, wished to do something that was forbidden by law (of course in the case of a man like himself what difficulty could there be?) and Alypius held out against him. He was offered a bribe, which he rejected with scorn. Threats were made against him, but these too he held in contempt. Everyone was amazed at so rare a spirit, "for he neither wanted the friendship nor feared the enmity of such a man."

It was in the course of his stay in Rome that Augustine completely detached himself from the beliefs of the Manichaeans. He confided to Alypius his anxieties, his troubles, and his doubts.

Soon his satirical spirit was turned against his coreligionists, whose puritanism now seemed hypocrisy to him. Even more than in Carthage, the Elect, who boasted of their austere fasts, took part in feasts on all occasions. Scandals broke out in the community. It was told that Faustus permitted himself many luxuries, and the Manichaean bishop in Rome was accused of dipping his hand into the till.

Greatly troubled, Augustine discreetly withdrew from their company, and interested himself even further in the endless discussions of the skeptical grammarians. He also made a deeper study of the thought of Cicero.

He had grown weary of going about giving lessons in the endless stretches of an indifferent Rome. Modesta and Adeodatus were still in Carthage, for he had no money to send for them. He tried to find a place as a functionary, not that he envied Alypius, for the courts his friend attended sat without recess. Was a lawyer's life not to be preferred? He thought he might register as a member of the bar but openings were few, and a powerful patron was needed for such a step.

To make a career in literature and philosophy was no less difficult. There were countless public readings and recitations on every street corner. Everyone was giving public readings, all the time and under all conditions, summer and winter, morning and night. Most of the sessions were held, it is true, in the afternoons, but there were the insatiables who tried to hold their audiences for the entire day and sometimes for several days in succession. Instead of fostering the love of literature, these public readings led to indigestion. To these professional and amateur windbags were added, in the bargain, those students whose teachers of rhetoric required them to prove their talent by public harangues.

Augustine dreamed of regular employment, for instance as a teacher of a rhetoric course in one of the State schools. To his disappointment he found all these positions in the Roman colleges were filled. Nevertheless, an opportunity was offered him—a contest was being held in Milan leading to the appointment of a teacher of rhetoric. He thought how wonderful it would be to receive a fixed salary, no longer to run about the streets giving lessons.

A friend introduced Augustine to Symmachus, the prefect of the city. A courteous man and a great noble, he was the peer of the great families and high-ranking officials of Rome, and played an active role in the life of an aristocracy which had outlived its best days and was frivolous and vain. A pagan like his friend Ausonius, the familiar of the emperor and of the Augusta, he was both a pedant and a wag.

A fine-looking man, Symmachus had enjoyed a brilliant career, having been in turn a *quaestor*, a pontiff, a proconsul and a governor of Africa. He was very sympathetic to Africans and retained a certain nostalgia for that seductive land. Now he was prefect of Rome and would soon be consul. He was also the cousin of the bishop of Milan, the future saint, Ambrose. Proud of his own writings, he was a great patron of letters, but he did not like Christians in general or his cousin Ambrose in particular.

If Augustine had been a Christian, Symmachus would not have sent him to Milan. But he knew—of course a prefect must know everything—that Augustine was a Manichaean. That was a mark in the man's favor, and it would be quite a joke to have a Manichaean professor of rhetoric appointed to Milan, hard by his cousin Ambrose, and near the young emperor, who was an Arian sympathizer. As a matter of fact, the Augusta, who was regent for her son, had just ordered a new persecution of the Manichaeans.

To make sure of Augustine's abilities, Symmachus suggested the subject of an improvised discourse which he wished the candidate to deliver in his presence. As he listened with benevolent nonchalance to his client, he could surely not have foreseen that this young professor, whose name he scarcely knew, would deliver the last blow to the gods and nail down the coffin of the old pagan world.

Symmachus decided to "guarantee the ability of the candidate to fill the chair in Milan which he was seeking."

Quite recently there had been a conflict in Milan between Bishop Ambrose and the court. At the beginning of her regency, the Empress Justina had taken care to be on excellent terms with Ambrose, thinking she would have need of his support against the claims of the usurper Maximus. But Theodosius had arrived in upper Italy and had persuaded Maximus to be content with ruling Gaul, Spain and Britain —in return the Emperor of the East had officially recognized Maximus as the third Augustus. The empress immediately manifested her Arian convictions, since this would assure her of the help of the Visigoths. Then, to placate the pagans, she had appointed Symmachus as prefect of Rome. The latter at once drew up a ringing appeal for the restoration of the statue and the altar of Victory to the assembly hall of the

Senate, an appeal which he himself considered to be an excellent bit of rhetoric.[1]

Ambrose launched a violent protest just as the court was on the point of authorizing the restoration of the statue, and threatened the emperor with excommunication if it took place. Nevertheless, the emperor continued to bestow marks of favor on Symmachus and to express his confidence in him on all occasions. Thus Symmachus thought it highly amusing to send Augustine the Manichaean to Milan as official teacher of rhetoric.

Now Augustine sent for his mistress and his son to come in all haste, and at the expense of the city of Milan he crossed Italy to his new post. He was thirty years old, matured by age, disillusionment and the difficulties of life. Suddenly he had become an important fuctionary, a prominent teacher in a great city which was the seat of the emperor of the West. He decided his behavior should be more correct, and that he would definitely reject Manichaeism since it was looked upon with disfavor by the half-Catholic, half-Arian court. He planned not to associate in the northern capital with any of the Manichaeans who had managed to remain, and in this he must persuade his friend Alypius to follow his example. For Alypius, it seems, had got himself appointed to the Milanese tribunal in order not to be separated from Augustine—probably, too, to escape the anger of the senator he had so bitterly offended.

Ambrose, in collision with the Arian Empress Justina, had the task of defending the Catholic Church. A true leader, a personage of considerable importance, and an orator of wide reputation, he came from an illustrious patrician family. His father had been prefect of Gaul, while he himself had been governor of the provinces of Aemilia and Liguria at the time he was acclaimed bishop, contrary to his own desires—something which frequently occurred in that epoch. Baptized (for he was still a catechumen), ordained priest and con-

secrated bishop in quick succession, he had resigned his civil
functions but continued to exercise his great influence.

Immediately on arriving in Milan, Augustine was installed
in his university class. What he heard of Ambrose intrigued
him, and he went to hear him preach, chiefly interested in his
reputation for eloquence. Later he asked to be allowed to pay
the bishop a courtesy visit. He was somewhat disappointed
in his welcome, for Ambrose received him with restraint.
Perhaps he distrusted this darkskinned African, appointed a
teacher in Milan upon the recommendation of Symmachus,
his cousin and personal enemy—no doubt this Carthaginian
was a Manichaean or a Donatist. And it could have been that
this counselor of emperors, the man who spoke as an equal
to the Augusta, felt some scorn for the young parvenu
rhetoric teacher, who could have seemed to him somewhat
pretentious. Thus he taught a lesson in humility to Augustine, perhaps without realizing it.

Although Ambrose's oratory was sober and devoid of
ornament, Augustine went regularly to hear him preach. He
attended these sermons as a sort of professional student of
the speaker's style, of his manner of introducing quotations,
of arranging his discourse. Soon he began to listen to him
with a pleasure mixed with astonishment. Ambrose was one
of the reformers of Christian preaching, and one of the first
to discover in the Old Testament, allegories and etymologi-
cal explanations which were sometimes a bit farfetched but
always ingenious. Suddenly Augustine saw the Bible as a
monument rich in symbolism and not as a collection of tales
that at times seemed to him immoral.

"I heard various passages in the Old Testament explained
most frequently by way of allegory, by which same passages I
was killed when I had taken them literally. Hence when
many passages in those books were explained spiritually, I
now blamed my own despair, in which I had believed that
the Law and the Prophets could in no way be upheld against
those who hated them and scoffed at them. Yet for all that

I did not think that the Catholic way must be held to by myself."

Nevertheless, he was anxious to discuss certain matters with Ambrose. But after his first semiofficial visit, Augustine was not able to see the bishop alone.

"I was unable to ask him what I wanted and in the way I wanted, for crowds of busy men, to whose troubles he was a slave, shut me away from both his ear and mouth."

It would seem that even if Ambrose stood in Augustine's path at a good moment, he personally did not do a great deal for the conversion of the future Father of the Church.

"Often when we were present—for no one was forbidden to enter, and it was not his custom to have whoever came announced to him—we saw him reading to himself, and never otherwise. After sitting for a long time in silence—who would dare to annoy a man so occupied?—we would go away."

Having lost one faith, Augustine had nevertheless not found another.

"After the manner of the Academics (as they supposedly are), I doubted everything and wavered in the midst of all things. Yet I resolved that the Manichaeans must be abandoned. Even in my skeptical period I did not see how I could persist in a sect above which I now placed many philosophers. But because these philosophers were without the saving name of Christ, I refused utterly to commit the cure of my soul's sickness to them."

When Augustine had escaped from Monica in so outrageous a fashion, his mother retired to Tagaste where she led a semicloistered existence, spending her time in prayer and fasting. When she learned that Augustine had finally found a good position, she decided to rejoin him at once. First, she could not make up her mind to lose him, and second, she wanted to rid him of the concubine who monopolized him and who was obviously unworthy of him. It should not be difficult to find a fine wife for her son, and the time had come for him to marry. She herself would take care of his household, and all would be for the best. She had great hopes of seeing him make a "fine" marriage.

Monica liquidated the little property she had received from Patricius and set out in the company of her elder son, Navigius, his two cousins, Rusticus and Lastidianus, and also Nebridius, an old friend of Augustine. This collective exodus was an African custom. One of their number had only to meet with success for all his family to collect around him, like flies around honey or moths around a lamp. Augustine seemed to have important connections and was perhaps even in a position to grant favors himself. No doubt it would be possible to live with him or with some of his associates.

His beginnings as a teacher of rhetoric in Milan had been brilliant. At the end of 384 he had been chosen to deliver the panegyric of Bauton, the victorious general against the Sarmatians on the Danube. This panegyric was delivered in the presence of an illustrious assembly which praised Augustine's eloquence despite his somewhat weak voice.

As soon as navigation was opened (traffic on the Mediterranean was closed between November and March), Monica and her company arrived in Milan, in the spring of 385. The atmosphere had become more and more strained between the Augusta Justina and Ambrose, the bishop. An Arian community had been formed in Milan, made up chiefly of Gothic soldiers. Justina and Valentinian associated with them openly, and the emperor, at his mother's persuasion, had ordered that the Arians be given a church outside the city walls. Ambrose put up strong opposition to this and the populace rose up to support him. The court backed down temporarily.

Augustine welcomed his mother with deference, for within he was remorseful at his treatment of her. On the other hand, things were soon at the breaking point between Monica and her son's mistress who lived in the house, together with young Adeodatus.

Augustine fell ill, for the cold, raw climate did not agree

with him. He was often obliged to stay away from his classes, choking with attacks of asthma, suffering from sore throat and loss of voice. His illnesses became so frequent that he worried about his future and even thought of applying for an administrative position in the government if his health did not improve.

Nebridius, a native of Carthage, had left his city, his mother, his rich estate, everything, in order to join Augustine. The latter sometimes reproached him gently for having cast all these things aside, and this made Nebridius violently angry. The years he had passed away from his young teacher, he said, had seemed to him years of exile. It was the same with Alypius.

Soon the good Romanianus, that enlightened patron of the arts, came to pay them a visit. He had journeyed to Milan to see a friend at court, for the levies now being extorted by the African government had almost ruined him. He had come to try to seek justice and was counting for help on the connections Augustine had already made at court. Augustine felt the time had come to try to repay the many favors he had received, and Alypius also joined in his efforts to aid Romanianus. Thus there formed around Augustine a small circle which was soon to become a phalanx.

One day when he was feeling particularly miserable, burning with fever and wracked with fits of coughing, and moreover faced with having to deliver an oration in praise of the emperor, he and his friends were walking along a street in Milan. He saw a poor beggar who, more than a little drunk, was laughing and jesting as though he were the happiest man in the world.

Augustine remarked to his friends that all his own painful labors until now had been for the purpose of attaining joy. Now this same joy of temporary happiness had been won by this beggar by means of a few coins received through public charity. Was such a sight not enough to persuade a man to cease his exertions and turn to the pleasures of an idle, care-free life, the *dolce vita?*

However, he began a friendship with Manlius Theodorus, a former proconsul at Carthage, who lived in retirement at his country place near Milan. Since his dismissal from office in 383, he had spent his time reading Plato and working in his garden. He was known as a Neoplatonist and had written a history of this philosophy and books on the parts of the soul and the origins of human life.

This friend, who was to become a consul some years later, held open house. He eagerly invited Augustine, whose conversation was so sparkling and unconstrained, to stay with him and entertain his guests. So Augustine spent many pleasant days with him on the shore of Lake Como in the same ease he had formerly enjoyed in the house of Romanianus.

It was then he made a marvelous discovery. Although he was a rhetorician, a teacher, a philosopher and had passed his thirtieth year, he had not yet read Plato and Plotinus. Manlius Theodorus lent him Plotinus' book *On the Beautiful.* Of Plotinus Augustine was to write in his *City of God:*

"Plotinus, developing the thought of Plato, asserts . . . that the rational soul . . . has no nature above it except that of God who fashioned the universe and created the soul itself. . . . He left no part of this creation without its appropriate peace, for in the last and least of all His living things the very entrails are wonderfully ordered—not to mention the beauty of birds' wings, and the flowers of the fields and the leaves of trees. And above the beauty of sky and earth is that of angels and of man."

It was after reading Plotinus that Augustine wrote:

"I was made certain that You exist, that You are infinite, although not diffused throughout spaces, either finite or infinite, that You are truly He who is always the same, with no varied parts and changing movements, and that all other things are from You, as is known by one single most solid proof, the fact that they exist."

He was now rid of the Epicureans, those men who refused to believe in the afterlife. He was no longer without hope of finding the Truth which is the nourishment of the soul. The Academics were wrong. The love of passing things was but a source of error and pain.

Augustine told the priest Simplicianus, the future bishop of Milan, that he had discovered Plato through Plotinus. The priest congratulated him, saying, "Those Platonist philosophers knew God and His Word."[2]

Shortly afterward one of his friends gave him the *Dialogues* of Plato, translated into Latin by the famous rhetorician Victorinus.

"I read, not indeed in these words but much the same thought, enforced by many varied arguments, that in the beginning was the Word, and the Word was with God, and the Word was God. The same was in the beginning with God. All things were made by Him, and without Him nothing was made. What was made in Him is life, and the life was the light of men. . . .

"I read that the soul of man, although it gives testimony of the light, is not itself the light, but the Word. God Himself, is 'the true light, which enlightens every man that comes into the world.'"

On reading Plato, Augustine entered a world he thought he did not know, and which nevertheless was familiar to him. Suddenly everything became almost miraculously easy to understand, to explain, and to hear.

Plato's writings were to open up to Augustine a new direction for his thoughts. Where do we find happiness? Augustine's answer was: in wisdom. What is wisdom? It is the possession of knowledge, a truth which satisfies our aspiration for beatitude. But Wisdom is one of the names of God. He is therefore the only One who can assure us happiness. Wisdom is Knowledge, or better, the possession of God. We must therefore advance on the path to Wisdom. In other words, we must advance toward God.

Augustine no longer refused to believe, but was eagerly in quest of faith. Nevertheless, although he saw where he must travel, he could not yet see his way.[3]

A born teacher, he at once expatiated on the Platonist ideas to his friends. His fiery denunciations turned them away from Manichaeism. He discussed with them a dream he had of founding a retreat away from troubles and turmoil, "a life of quiet, apart from the crowd." Each would put what he possessed into a common fund in a spirit of sincere friendship so that it could no longer be said, "this thing belongs to that man and another to that." He counted that they would be ten in number, including Romanianus "who has always been very close to me." Since Romanianus' wealth exceeded that of the others, his wishes in the matter would carry much weight.

But the friends began to ask if their wives would permit such a life—for some of them were already married. As a result, the beautiful plan, so carefully worked out, went up in smoke.

Augustine had confided in his mother that he was no longer a Manichaean, although not a Catholic, and added that he had recently become interested in Plato's philosophy through Manlius Theodorus. Monica responded to this in a manner that showed her confidence in God, saying "that before she departed this life she would see me a faithful Catholic." And there she stopped.

"This much she said to me. But to you, O fountain of mercies, she multiplied her prayers and tears, so that you would speed your help and enlighten my darkness. More zealously still, she would hasten to the church, and she would hang on the words of Ambrose as on 'a fountain of water springing up into life everlasting.' For she loved that man as though he were an angel of God."

Monica, who had taken over the material and moral care of the household, could now show her love for her brilliant son and her faith in his future. She was in no doubt as to the ultimate reason for this sojourn in Italy. During her voyage from Africa, a violent storm had arisen and she had reassured the sailors and promised them they would reach port safe and sound. All in all she was a stalwart woman, and once more Augustine felt like a small boy in her presence.

Although Ambrose had not been too warm in his reception of the teacher of rhetoric, he showed much interest in Monica. He knew her to be a fervent Christian, although doubtless a bit superstitious and given to African customs such as carrying to the martyrs' tombs baskets of bread and wine. When she appeared at the entrance of one of the basilicas in Milan with her basket, the doorkeeper had barred her way, saying the bishop had prohibited such practices. Monica had accepted this in an obedient and respectful manner and had asked to be allowed to see Ambrose who explained that such offerings went back to pagan traditions and should be abandoned.

She listened eagerly to every word that came from Ambrose's lips, counting on him in some obscure fashion to help her with her rebellious son. The bishop was well-disposed toward her because of her fervent piety, and when, one day, he met Augustine, he congratulated him on having such a mother.

In meantime the teacher was not unmindful of his career —far from it. He was even listening with more interest to Monica's words of counsel.

Between his mother and his mistress, Augustine's life had become impossible. Yet Alypius advised him against marriage. Was it because he would be better off without marriage? Or did he no longer love Modesta? Moreover, if Augustine married, he and Alypius could not carry out their plan to live together in the unbroken leisure and zeal for learning they had so long desired.

Alypius was living a chaste life. He had known "the bitter pleasures of the flesh" in early manhood, but had soon turned away from them. Now he distrusted sensual pleasure and lived in complete continence.

When Augustine, still a slave to his passions, questioned him on this subject, Alypius answered that he regarded such pleasures as infamous. To which Augustine retorted that many men who were married still faithfully loved and kept their friends and cherished wisdom.

"Caught fast in a disease of the flesh with its deadly sweetness, I dragged along my chains and was fearful of being loosed from them. As if my wound had been struck, I repelled his good and persuasive words, as I would a hand unlocking my chains. . . . He marveled that I, whom he esteemed in no slight way, would stick so fast in the birdlime of that pleasure as to affirm that I could never lead a celibate life. When I saw that he was astonished at me, I urged in my defense that there was a great difference between what he had taken quickly and furtively, which he could scarcely remember and therefore might scorn easily and without regret, and my long-continued pleasure. Moreover, if the honored name of matrimony were added to it, he ought not to wonder why I could not despise this way of life."

When Augustine was alone he could see he was on the wrong track from every point of view. He no longer had a desire to reach out for any good fortune that might come his way or to seize those opportunities he had hitherto grasped so eagerly.

With Alypius and Nebridius, his two bosom friends, he vacillated in heart and mind. "Ardent seekers after a happy life and subtle critics of the most difficult questions, we were three men in want, who were sighing out their needs to one another. . . . Darkness confronted us. Groaning we turned away, and we said, 'How long shall these things last?'"[4]

Monica was making great efforts to get her son married. It was not her habit to delay in carrying out her projects. He must first of all get rid of the troublesome "concubine."

A drama took place in his home which Augustine, in his *Confessions*, tries to gloss over or at least to tone down, but which must have been very painful for him; his grief, moreover, is apparent in certain of his phrases.

Monica was the author of this drama. She argued that "this woman" was harmful to his reputation and to his career. Besides, the conflicts in authority between Augustine's mother and his mistress had become insupportable. Augustine had to choose between his mother and his future on one hand and, on the other, this slave's daughter whose origins were obscure and whom he had picked up, no one knows how, on the streets of Carthage.

There could be no question of her son regularizing so unworthy a liaison. Monica was the widow of a decurion, and herself the daughter of an excellent middle-class family. Her son was fast rising on the social ladder, and the time had come for him to choose a wife. One heard no word these days about his being an "African," and the best families in Milan were happy to welcome him to their home.

"The woman with whom I was wont to share my bed was torn from my side as an impediment to my marriage. My heart still clung to her; it was pierced and wounded within me, and the wound drew blood from it. She returned to Africa, vowing that she would never know another man, and leaving with me our natural son."

Was this so simple or so natural? The "intruder" went back to Africa, leaving behind her everything she loved. Moreover, since she was a Catholic, she was going to a convent, there to finish out her days. She left heartbroken but without uttering a cry either to the man she loved or to the child she had borne him.

Now that the way was clear, Augustine's marriage must be arranged at once. After several disappointments, Monica fixed her choice on a young Christian girl, for she thought that Augustine's marriage would lead him to baptism.

Unfortunately the girl was too young. She lacked two years

of the age of consent; he would have to wait. Perhaps it would have been better to have given a delay of grace to the undesirable concubine. But it was too late for that.

Unfortunately, Augustine had taken no vow of chastity. Patricius' blood was in his veins, and he lost no time in taking a new mistress.

"I procured another woman, but not, of course, as a wife. By her my soul's disease would be fostered and brought safe, as it were, either unchanged or in a more intense form, under the convoy of continued use into the kingdom of marriage. Not yet healed within me was that wound which had been made by the cutting away of my former companion. After intense fever and pain, it festered, and it still caused me pain, although in a more chilling and desperate way."

The discussions with Alypius and Nebridius continued. All three sought certitude. Augustine had separated his friends from Manichaeism, but what could he offer them in its place?

"If we were immortal and lived in perpetual bodily pleasure without any fear of loss, why should we not be happy, and what else would we ask for?" he one day said.

Nothing would have prevented them from adopting the theories of Epicurus except the certainty, which they all shared, that the soul lives on after death and would be rewarded or punished in accordance with its deeds on earth.

The uncertain state of his health caused Augustine much concern. Distracted at his asthmatic attacks and his spells of weakness, Monica consulted the best doctor in Milan. The air of the city, it seemed, was definitely bad for African lungs.

Moreover, Augustine could not sleep. He was unhappy and harassed by remorse. Where was Modesta? How was she living and was she really unhappy? He did not doubt that she was, and he both pitied and missed her. Besides, the new concubine was unbearable.

In addition, alarming news was coming from Africa. Gildo, who had been appointed the previous year as Roman general in Carthage, had put a complete stop to any persecution of the Donatists. More than that, he had placed behind Optatus, Donatist bishop of Thamugadi (Timgad), the support of his troops, and these were reinforced by the Circumcellion rebels to exploit the people and crush the Catholic minorities.

Gildo was counting on the Donatist bishops to secure and maintain his power. Within a short time he attained his object and was long to wield mastery over the country. It was revulsion against his incredible abuses which hastened Augustine's evolution toward the Church.

The latter's career was now at a standstill. Often his voice failed him and his Carthaginian accent was mocked by his fellow teachers—and sometimes even by his students. His anxiety and disarray increased; he was engulfed by great waves of melancholy.

The affairs of the court were also at a low ebb. By recruiting mercenaries into the imperial armies, the weak Empress Justina had enabled the barbarians to enter the Empire peacefully and to corrode it from within. They were soon everywhere, in every strategic post, and the Augusta did nothing to forestall them. Persuaded by his mother and by the Goths, who were converts to Arianism, the emperor promulgated an edict of toleration toward the Arians, and required that one of the churches of Milan be turned over to the schismatics.

Ambrose refused, and the situation deteriorated. The Gothic mercenaries (who were Arians) were detailed to keep order around the church in question. The bishop brought all his authority to bear on the Roman soldiers in Milan to have them disobey the imperial command, and this resulted in conflicts within the army between the two opposing factions. The emperor decided to have recourse to force to bring the belligerent bishop to terms; he was to be arrested if necessary. Whereupon Ambrose immediately transformed his basilica into a fortress and entrenched himself inside with his priests and some of the faithful.

"The emperor," he thundered, "can dispose of my life, but

I will not betray Our Lord nor His Church. I am ready to bear whatever torture the demon's malice may devise and I ask to die on the steps of the altar."

A number of the faithful asserted they were ready to die with him. Among these was Monica.

Time passed slowly in the immense fortified building. Fearing boredom, discouragement, perhaps desertions, Ambrose had an idea. To occupy the faithful and the priests, to pass the hours, he had them chant hymns and canticles alternately as was done by certain Christians of the Eastern Church. The liturgical chant was thus introduced into the West, and it was first heard in the Milan basilica.

Finally, on Good Friday, April 3, 386, the court gave in.

Augustine was overwhelmed when he joined his mother after her incarceration. She had grown thin and hollow-eyed, yet burned with the fire of her intense faith. With deep attention he listened as she recounted her experiences.

Augustine was a born musician, and for him God was the Musician of the universe. Later he himself would hear the singing which Monica described.

"How greatly did I weep during hymns and canticles, keenly affected by the voices of your sweet-singing Church! Those voices flowed into my ears, and your truth was distilled into my heart."

No one had been more stirred than Augustine during those troubled months. He had been deeply moved by the Church's misfortunes.

Finally a miracle took place. Ambrose discovered the bodies of two martyrs, Protasius and Gervasius.

"At that time You revealed by a vision to Your prelate the place in which the bodies of the martyrs Protasius and Gervasius lay hidden, which for so many years You had stored away uncorrupted in Your secret treasure house. In due time You would bring them forth from that place so as to restrain the mad rage of a woman, yes, a woman of royal rank. When they were discovered and dug up, and with fitting honors transferred into the Ambrosian basilica, not only were those tormented by unclean spirits healed, while those same demons confessed themselves, but also a certain citizen, very well known throughout the city, who had been blind for years . . . begged to be admitted so that he might touch the bier with his handkerchief. . . . When he had done this and touched the cloth to his eyes, they were immediately opened. From that place the story spread abroad. . . . From there, the mind of that hostile woman, although not turned to sound belief, was yet restrained from the fury of persecution."

Now and then Augustine held converse on the subject of Plato with Simplicianus, the old priest who years before had converted Ambrose. Simplicianus spoke to Augustine of Plato's translator, the learned pagan Victorinus, who had turned to Christ in his old age. On the day of his baptism, the famous rhetorician had mounted to the elevated place reserved for the catechumens in the Roman Forum. There, like the humblest of the converts, he had made his profession of faith: Plato leads to Christ.[5]

Sometime later, as Augustine was talking with Alypius, a certain Ponticianus from Africa came to see them. In the course of their conversation, Ponticianus spoke admiringly of the holiness of Antony and his monks who lived in the Egyptian desert. As he spoke, Augustine marveled and a familiar feeling pervaded him. Then the visitor from Africa spoke of two officers he had met in Germany who had been so struck by what they heard of Antony's sacrifices that they determined to give themselves to God, and had influenced their affianced brides to do the same.

"Ponticianus told us this story, and as he spoke, You, O Lord, turned me back upon myself. You took me from behind my own back, where I had placed myself because I did not wish to look upon myself. You stood me face to face with myself, so that I might see how foul I was, how deformed and defiled, how covered with stains and sores. I looked, and I was filled with horror, but there was no place for me to flee away from myself. If I tried to turn my gaze from myself, he still went on with the story that he was telling, and once again You placed me in front of myself, and thrust me before my own eyes, so that I might find out my iniquity and hate it. I knew what it was, but I pretended not to."

Ponticianus expressed surprise at seeing the Epistles of St. Paul on a table near which he sat. Augustine replied that he was making a study of Holy Scripture, as also of Plato and Plotinus.

Augustine thought how many years had flown since his nineteenth year when his reading of Cicero's *Hortensius* had aroused in him a zeal for wisdom. For at least eleven years he had striven on this path, yet still he delayed to despise earthly pleasures and devote himself entirely to the search. "For the bare search for wisdom, even when it is not actually found, was preferable to finding treasures and earthly kingdoms and to bodily pleasures."

Ponticianus departed, and Augustine remained alone with Alypius. He realized to what point he had sunk beneath "the burden of vanity," a sleep of the mind from which it does not wake. He saw, however, that the state of a man awake is better than when he is asleep. What was the law of sin if not the force of habit, which dominates and carries us away despite ourselves?

Alypius was astounded at the trouble and anguish he saw in his friend's face.

"What is the trouble with us?" Augustine cried out. "What is this? What did you hear? The unlearned rise up and take heaven by storm, and we, with all our erudition but empty of heart, see how we wallow in flesh and blood! Are we ashamed to follow because they have gone on ahead of us?"

Alypius made no answer. Augustine was speaking in an extraordinary tone of voice; his brow, his eyes, his cheeks, the color of his face told more than the words he stammered out so harshly. He rose suddenly and left the house for the small garden outside. He needed to be alone, yet Alypius followed him. They sat down as far as they could from the house, at the end of the garden.

Augustine knew that all he needed to do to be delivered was to *will* it, firmly and finally, "not to turn and toss, now here, now there, a struggling half-maimed will, with one part rising upward and another falling downward."

Thus, he thought, when his soul gave a command to his bodily members, they obeyed him. For example, he willed to move his hand and it moved; scarcely had the order been given by the soul when the hand acted. But now the soul gave a command to itself and was not obeyed. Was this not something monstrous?[6]

Augustine felt that he was ready to attain his goal; he almost touched it. But he had always drawn back; a Manichaean, he had never willed to make the break. For him, the accomplishment of faith demanded a total renunciation of his former life. Pleasures plucked at his "fleshly garment," and seemed to be saying, "Do not cast us off!"

He knew he was being held back by the vainest of ephemeral joys, by the most deceptive forces, by things he had valued for so long. They picked at him and said, "From that moment no longer will this thing and that be allowed to you, forever and ever." They delayed the effort Augustine was making to extricate himself. He felt himself paralyzed, and heard the tyrannical voice insisting, "Do you think that you can live without them?"

Alypius sat motionless, silently awaiting the outcome of Augustine's extraordinary agitation. Then he saw his friend rise and go farther away, trying to restrain his tears. Glued to his place, Alypius watched as Augustine cast himself on the ground beneath a fig tree and give way to a storm of weeping.

For the first time, Augustine was *praying*.

"And You, O Lord, how long? Will You be angry forever?

Remember not our past iniquities. How long, how long? To-morrow and tomorrow? Why not now? Why not in this very hour an end to my uncleanness?"

It was then he heard a voice that seemed to come from a nearby house. It was the voice of a girl or of a child, and it chanted over and over the same words.

"Take up and read. Take up and read."

Again he heard these words repeated, and began to wonder if they were part of a song or a game. He could not remember if they were, but ceasing to weep, he rose and hurried back to the spot where Alypius was sitting.

There he found the Epistles of St. Paul, where he had left them. Augustine opened the book and read the lines on which his eyes first fell.

"Not in rioting and drunkenness, not in chambering and impurities, not in strife and envying; but put you on the Lord Jesus Christ, and make not provision for the flesh and its concupiscences."

He read no farther, but turned to Alypius with so peaceful a mien his friend guessed what had happened. He wished to see what Augustine had read and continued to the passage that followed. It read: "Now him that is weak in the faith take unto you."

Immediately thereafter the two men, brimming with joy, went to find Monica to tell her what had occurred. She was astounded but filled with exultation, and asked them to repeat to her their story in all its details.

It was clear to Augustine he must renounce everything—his projected marriage, his ambitions and the sensual delights which had meant so much to him. In his eyes this was a necessary step to be carried out immediately. Thus, at thirty-three years of age, he broke suddenly and finally with the world and its pleasures.

Vacation time was near, and he would leave his students at the end of the course. The twenty days he had to wait

seemed very long, but he could not do otherwise than continue his classes until the end of the year.

His health needed attention, for he was spending many
nights without sleep because of bronchitis and asthma. His
voice was almost gone; he breathed with difficulty. It was
even feared that his lungs were affected.

Where would he spend the summer with his friends? He
had no money.

Verecundus, a friend of Nebridius and like him a teacher
of grammar, owned a villa called Cassiciacum on the outskirts of Milan. He proposed to Augustine that he make it
his home for the summer in exchange for supervising the
labor in the fields. There he could meditate with Alypius
and Nebridius, all of whom would be at leisure. Augustine
could continue giving lessons to Licentius, the son of Romanianus and another young man, named Trygetius, in order
to earn enough for his daily needs.

Thus the community was constituted. Verecundus was unhappy at not being able to join his friends, but he was
married and had other duties in Milan. Other than Monica,
who ran the household, Augustine objected violently to the
presence of any woman.

This arrangement was to continue for the duration of the
vacation. Augustine wrote to Romanianus, who had returned
to Tagaste, begging him to join them as soon as possible.

"Bereft of my father, your friendship has consoled me.
You have always aided me with your fortune. Your affection
and your benefactions have made me a person of importance.
You watched over me from childhood and encouraged me
in my first flight, in the delights of seeking the truth, and
in the happiness of finding it. All is your work. I hope that
the desire for a life like the one I wish, will enter your heart
also."[7]

Augustine had decided no longer to derive happiness or
joy in the world or in those things "sought with fleshly eyes
under that outward sun."

But he had not reached the end of his difficulties.

"Your Word, eternal Truth, surpassingly above the highest parts of Your universe, raised up there to Himself those who had been brought low. Amid the lower parts He had built for Himself out of our clay a lovely dwelling, in which He would protect from themselves those ready to become submissive to Him, and bring them to Himself. He heals their swellings, and nourishes their love, so that they may not go on further in self-confidence, but rather become weak. For at their feet they see the Godhead, weak because of our participation in our 'coats of skin,' and in their weariness they may cast themselves upon It, while It arises and lifts them up.

"But I had other thoughts: I conceived my Lord Christ only as a man of surpassing wisdom, whom no other man could equal. . . . But what mystery was contained within those words, 'The Word was made flesh,' I could not conceive."

Chapter Five

CASSICIACUM
386-387

At "beautiful Cassiciacum, where far from the world's turmoil we found rest," Augustine gathered his disciples around him as Socrates had done centuries before. He also began a definitive stage in the probing of his own mind and heart, for he had taken the child's song in the garden and the words of St. Paul's epistle as a Sign. And doubtless he was haunted by sorrowful memories and knew pangs of the remorse he had felt ever since Modesta went away. For him Cassiciacum was a refuge, also a halting place where he could meditate and try to rebuild his world, to write "Finis" to a chapter of his life.

It was a beautiful house—simple and peasant-like, the summer home of a middle-class Milanese—set upon a hill and surrounded by mountains. In the distance could be seen Monte Rosa and a range of snow-covered Alpine peaks which joined the Apennies to the south; overhead, the clear pure sky of northern Italy. Such was the earthly paradise praised by Licentius when he wrote of "the suns that went down among the lofty Italian mountains."

Alypius was free, for he had resigned from his post. On the other hand Nebridius was still teaching grammar in Milan and could come only from time to time. He was a gentle and discreet man who avoided anything that might trouble the serene equilibrium of his mind and who wished to take advantage of any leisure he might have to read and meditate, "to drink of wisdom."

Living with them was the boy Adeodatus, now twelve years of age, whose "power of mind surpassed many grave and learned men." Also Navigius, who was suffering from a liver complaint, Augustine's cousins Rusticus and Lastidianus, and finally his students Trygetius, who had just quitted the army, and Licentius, the son of Romanianus. Licentius was unbridled, petulant and sarcastic by nature—and an impenitent pagan who in the discussions at Cassiciacum always espoused the opposing side. He was also a poet and in the evenings liked to recite the verses he had composed.

Several days after his arrival, Augustine suffered a relapse —an abominable attack of asthma—and thought he would die. Fortunately the alarm was false, for the summer was dry and he quickly recovered. Soon he was able to be about again and his convalescence was a double one, for it also brought him more peace of soul.

Now each one busied himself with arranging his daily schedule. Monica managed the house: "She took care of us as though she had been mother to us all, and she served us as though she had been daughter to all of us."

The mornings were given over to lessons, Augustine explaining Vergil and giving courses in grammar and rhetoric. The afternoons were devoted to free discussion, often so passionate that it continued far into the night. The spirit of an ancient world seemed to pervade these hours at Cassiciacum as young and ardent minds strove "to unfold their wings in order to ascend to God."

Augustine wished a careful record of these conversations to be kept, doubtless because he felt the need to mark down, day by day, the evolution of his thinking. The questions and opinions of the young men about him helped him in his own laborious search. The remarks of each were to be set down in his own words, and the whole would serve as "Augustine's journal" in the course of his conversion.

The dialogues *Against the Academics*, *On Order*, and *On the Happy Life* are important in that through them we follow the development of Augustine's thought. The importance he himself attached to them is proved by the fact he caused stenographic reports to be made. Notaries, or scribes, were present during the talks, jotting them down in abbreviated form and transcribing them afterward. Progress had indeed been made since Socrates' time, for he, like Plato, had to rely on memory alone.

It is apparent from these records that Augustine's thinking was in a state of flux. That the Academics left life without a meaning, he was convinced. What was the good of wisdom and human intelligence if there were no afterlife? The intellect is made for truth; but to discover truth, a divine authority is needed to show the way.

"What I did there by way of literary work, which was already in Your service, although during this period as it were of rest it still breathed forth the school of pride, my books bear witness, both the ones that resulted from discussions with those present there and the ones made by myself alone."

Augustine allowed everyone to take part in the conversations—even the child Adeodatus, who was very intelligent. All, like himself, were seeking happiness through Wisdom.

Licentius said: "We can be happy just in looking for truth."

And Navigius: "To be happy is to spend one's life in the search for truth."

Trygetius thought more was needed: "Seeking is not in itself a stable state. One must arrive at perfection."

Augustine asked his disciples this question: "Are we all obliged to know the truth?"

All answered in the affirmative.

Augustine defined the happy life as "one in conformity with what is best and most perfect in man. Now there is nothing of such excellence in man as that part of the soul which is obeyed by all other parts, namely, reason."

He was not attracted by what is compassionate and merciful in Christianity, rather by austerity, war against error, combat against the enemies of God. Overnight, Augustine became a man of the Old Testament. This explains his power in the midst of a worn-out society whose decay was scarcely concealed by its refined culture.

The three volumes *Against the Academics* were addressed to Romanianus who still remained in Africa where his business interest had been placed in jeopardy by Gildo and the Circumcellions who ravaged the province. When he sent Romanianus the books, Augustine wrote that he would still be caught in the net of "human snares" had it not been for the lung trouble which obliged him to leave his school in Milan; this sickness had been "the stroke of fortune" which led him "to the bosom of true philosophy." And he added: "It was this which turned me away from the superstition into which I dragged you down with myself."

He felt he had to convert the good Romanianus as soon as possible. In the second chapter of the second book of *Against the Academics*, Augustine enumerates the favors Romanianus has showered on him, and also tells him of his own conversion (the *Confessions* were not written until fourteen years later).

Against the Academics is written in a loose, relaxed and lively style, with many digressions. The report of subtle dialectical exchanges is interspersed with accounts of daily happenings—such as mice getting into the room where the disciples were sleeping, cockfights in the barnyard, Alypius' arrival from Milan, or a night of insomnia.

Throughout this work Augustine is trying to convince an interlocutor, even when the latter does not answer; besides, this interlocutor is almost always himself. Augustine is writing for himself, trying to persuade by piling up arguments and syllogisms, developing his prodigious power of dialectic.

"It is hard to be happy when one does not know the last word or the why and how," he wrote to Nebridius in Milan. "We see in beings particles of beauty, of truth, of goodness. This implies that our intelligence is in relationship with Being Itself, Unity Itself, Truth Itself, Goodness Itself. This relationship consists in participating in knowledge which is in God Himself, but it does not necessarily include the immediate intuition of God. That cannot be accomplished without the help of sensible knowledge."

Augustine knew that reason alone was not enough to deliver us from darkness. He humbly avowed: "God permitted the truth of His divine intelligence to lower itself into a human body, to inspire souls and give them strength to look toward the heavenly country. I have not been able to do this but I am only thirty-three, and I do not despair of one day arriving at this point."

Alypius one day asked him to talk otherwise than by asking questions. Augustine agreed conditionally. He recalled Plato's two worlds—the world of the intellect which is the seat of truth and the visible world which is accessible to the senses. The first, he said, is the true world, the second is a semblance traced on the image of the first. From the luminous heights of the first descends the light that illumines the human soul; from the second arise the opinions that trouble the minds of foolish men.

Despite this apparent certitude, he had great difficulty in covering the ground step by step. He wrote to Alypius, who had gone off on a journey: "The Academics implanted in my mind the probability that man is here below to seek truth. To these same Academics it also seemed probable that he would never find it."

He undertook a minute refutation of Academic skepticism —going over a point again and again, backward and forward. The *rational* justification of the idea of Truth, the foundation of the doctrine of wisdom, was to form the essential basis of his philosophy. To make progress on this road, the contribution of the "liberal sciences" was essential. Against the skeptics he brought the argument that there are many absolutely certain truths which man is capable of knowing and of having no doubts about. This truth is attained particularly through the study of the sciences and especially of mathematics.[1]

How searing was this quest! In the interplay of minds that continued on the grassy sward beneath the chestnut tree at Cassiciacum much anguish was expressed.

On every page reported of these conversations we read the word "Truth." Truth was what Augustine desired, sought, contemplated, consulted with others about, which he himself clarified and expatiated upon, and for which he hoped.

"Truth is the affirmation of what is. The Word of God is Truth. If one considers the Father as the principle of the Son and the Son as the image of the Father, the Son is Truth.

"There are truths to which it is impossible to give the appearance of error. Every man should be happy; man tends toward happiness. One can see from the direction of his efforts where each one thinks that happiness lies. The philosopher seeks it in what is true—his happiness lies in the discovery of Truth. From the very fact he denies it, truth affirms itself and is fed by what claims to destroy it. For example, either the soul is immortal or it can die. If there are four elements, there are not five; these are modest certainties, but sufficient, to show that truth exists.

"But what if you are mistaken?

"If I am mistaken, then I am mistaken. Everyone who knows that he is in doubt about something, knows a truth, and in regard to this he knows that he is certain. Therefore he is certain about a truth. Consequently everyone who doubts if there be a truth, knows a true thing which he does not doubt; nor is there any true thing which is not true by truth."

Augustine used this first form of *cogito* to prove in turn the certainty of Truth, of the existence of God, the im-

mortality of the soul, and the image of the Trinity within
ourselves.

But he still doubted, although he believed that he was
saved.

"The mind attached to earthly things does not enter the
haven of Wisdom unless the wind of ill fortune or some
happy chance pushes him into it."

This shows to what extent he had been impressed by the
arguments of the skeptics, and also how great was his need
of being delivered from their influence. It was as though he
were in a desert, dying of thirst. He was hoping with all his
strength.

"In writing *Against the Academics* I was delivered, I was
freed. I escaped from this obsession; I had to take the skeptics
by the horns. What better use could I make of my freedom
than to purge my mind of skepticism? I was a child in
philosophy, but this childhood was full of promises for me.
I had a foretaste of eternal things."

When he was alone he read the Gospels and the Acts of
the Apostles. "So soon as certain books had poured on me
the perfumes of Arabia and fed my little flame with drops
of their precious oil, a tremendous flame glowed forth and
its light spread within me."

Of the fruitfulness of this retreat at Cassiciacum Augustine
wrote in his *Confessions:* "When will there be time to com-
memorate all the great benefits that You showed to us at that
time! . . . My memory calls me back, and it becomes sweet
to me, O Lord, to confess to You by what inward goads You
mastered me, and how You leveled me down by making low
the mountains and the hills of my thoughts, how You made
straight my crooked paths and smoothed the rough, and how
You likewise subdued my heart's brother, Alypius himself, to
the name of Your Only-begotten Son, our Lord and Savior
Jesus Christ. For at first he disdained to put that name into
our writings, but wished rather to have them partake of the

style of the schools which the Lord had now broken down, than of the simplicity of the Gospel."

Augustine could now prepare himself for baptism. No longer would he sell to young men the art of disguising the truth. Thus when the vacation came to an end (and thanks to funds sent from Africa by Romanianus), he sent his resignation to "those in Milan." They were now free to arrange for another teacher of rhetoric.

Augustine wrote to Bishop Ambrose to make known to him his "present intention" and to ask what books of the Scriptures he should read to the end that he might prepare himself for baptism.

Ambrose recommended the prophet Isaiah who foretold so plainly the Gospel mysteries. Augustine obediently began to read this book, but he did not understand it and so he put it aside until "I was better accustomed to the Lord's mode of speech."

Soon autumn came with its long evenings spent by the burning hearth. The weather was cold and humid. On November 13, the anniversary of Augustine's birth, they were all together, with the exception of Alypius who was in Milan. They would try to spend the winter at Cassiciacum, and on certain days the scribe would come to take notes of a dialogue, probably prepared in advance.

These days of research, of struggle against the others and against himself, were of great usefulness to Augustine despite his cruel uncertainties.

"The central problem," he wrote in his book *On Order*, "is happiness, the possession of a Truth which directs our hope toward beatitude. God is the only possession who can assure our happiness. Wisdom then is the knowledge of God, and this Wisdom cannot be attained at one stroke.

"What is needed is rigorous discipline, a regulated mode of life, moral order, and moral and intellectual studies. We must live rightly, pray rightly and study rightly.

"The soul strives toward God. Wisdom is of supernatural

origin and is a gift of Grace; hence the necessity of prayer. But the constructive effort of reason is also needed for the attainment of philosophical truth; then meditation spreads to the mystical plane and at the same time remains intellectual."

It was only much later, in his *Confessions*, that Augustine admitted the persistent anxiety which pursued him at Cassiciacum. When he was alone he expressed his hope and his despair in writing the most heartrending of all his books, *The Soliloquies*. He wrote *The Soliloquies* in the form of the dialectical exercise which came naturally to him, asking himself questions and replying as if there were two persons, Reason and himself, despite the fact he was terribly alone.

"Grant first that I may beg the right things of You, then make me worthy to be heard and finally grant that I be delivered. Faith, hope and charity are needed for man to come to God.

"My God, let me come to know You.

"Do you know that you exist?

"I know it.

"How do you know it?

"I do not know.

"Weep if it be that in this mortal life you shall never know anything more than you know now."

For forty-five years his writings were to reflect his anxiety to "know more." He could now say:

"The desire to live happily is common to all men, good or bad. But happiness, real happiness, lies in seeing and loving God."

He addressed God as "You Whom evil cannot harm." This was to be his future incontrovertible argument against Manichaeism.

To his search for truth he had sacrificed everything—pleasure, honors, ambition. He prayed fervently, but his object eluded him. Torn and unhappy as he was, he wished to spare his disciples the anguish and bitterness he knew. Therefore he prepared for them lessons in grammar, dialectics and mathematics,[2] accustoming these young men to move in the world of ideas. These studies, he believed, would introduce them little by little into the climate of suprasensible reality.

"Man thinks. He is not satisfied with the manifold sensations he feels, nor with the material things piled up in his memory. His mind moves on to the phenomena which arise in his conscience, and he says, 'I exist,' 'That is a beautiful statue,' 'This is a good action,' 'I know,' 'I think,' 'I doubt.'

"I would not think if I did not know what Being is. Being, knowing, truth and beauty exist in a pure state. Their synthesis is supreme reality."

Then Augustine would fall again into despair: "Why do you torture me? I am already worn out with much weeping. Only He I burn to behold knows the hour of my cure; I trust myself into His hands. Hold back your tears, you have shed too many, and this works ill in sick lungs. The lost are not so abandoned that they may not cry out to God to deliver them as quickly as may be from the pleasures of the flesh."

Augustine wrote the two books of *On Order* with his disciples. It was difficult to comprehend, let alone to perceive an immutable Order in the governing of the universe. A soul too concerned with a multiplicity of objects could understand nothing of the universe, for its beauty consists in the Unity that gives it its name. "It is not possible to solve without proper preparation a question of this kind. You are like a schoolmaster trying to teach syllables to a child who does not know his alphabet."

Another problem considered briefly in the second book of *On Order* was the existence of evil. For the first time Augustine applied his axe to the Manichaean structure which later he would endeavor to demolish. But here again he came face to face with the ghost of his youth and he still bore the scars of his ancient wounds. He was as yet too sensitive to all these things to get to the bottom of the problem of evil.

The last work written at Cassiciacum, *On Order*, was dedi-

cated to Manlius Theodorus who had guided him to Plato.
As Marrou says:

"More literary and less scientific in style, this work contrasted the early dialogues on Cicero and Plato held at Cassiciacum with dialogues which went on later. The characters
of those who took part in them are defined, and the contribution of each personage is recognizable. In a word, their
'dramatic' element is notable.

"These dialogues are the notation of conversations which
really took place. They were also the means of introducing
the reader to the handling of ideas, of abstract argument, of
accustoming him little by little to the methods of metaphysical research. This dialectical joust had therefore the value of
an exercise in mental gymnastics: 'All the long circuits we
have made have no other aim than to give you flexibility,'
said Augustine."

He was now convinced there were only two motives for
believing and knowing anything—authority and reason. "As
for myself I am persuaded no one can depart in any manner
from the authority of Jesus Christ."[3]

Chapter Six

THE RETURN
387–390

His pupils had left him, Trygetius to reenter the army and Licentius to install himself in Rome. Augustine was left with his mother, his son, his brother Navigius, his dear Alypius, and Evodius. For each of them Cassiciacum had been a turning point. They had decided to put aside "literary culture" and to turn to religious studies. But this decision had not been reached all at once by means of any outward revelation. On the contrary, the events of the eighteen months in Milan had brought about this decision very slowly in the manner of a cloud gathering on the horizon, at a time when Augustine was tortured by metaphysical anguish.

Now at Cassiciacum rhetoric and literature were proscribed and all the discussions were on philosophical problems. Cassiciacum became a sort of "lay monastery" where along Socratic lines Augustine and his friends exercised that spiritual discipline which leads to the knowledge of God.

The beautiful prayers at the beginning of *The Soliloquies* are not yet completely Christian, yet they show a tremendous effort to ascend toward God. In them Augustine implores the boon of wisdom and outlines his future doctrine concerning grace; with rare perception he foreshadows the direction his future thinking is to take.

Wisdom is the fruit of culture obtained on the one hand

by man's efforts, but on the other it is of supernatural origin. It is the effect of grace—hence the necessity of prayer.

"Pray not for riches and honors that are perishable but to obtain that which makes us happy and good, namely Wisdom."

From this time forward Augustine affirmed the necessity of *believing* in order to *understand.* In his eyes this essential requirement marked the importance of the religious element in the search for wisdom.

There was also the moral aspect. It was necessary to renounce concupiscence and the "tumult of vice"; to abstain from the pleasures of the flesh, those things that "entice the belly and the mouth"; to avoid undue attention to the body, luxury, a vain interest in games, too much sleep and idleness. Any desire for glory or political ambitions should be cast aside. In this way one could worship God and live in faith, hope and charity.

Finally, there was the intellectual aspect: the way of reason was to be followed for the purpose of attaining to possession of God and rising to contemplation of Him. All culture should be subordinated to this end.

The cloud had lifted, the storm had shaken the earth, and now Augustine knew he was free to move forward. He felt he was ready to receive baptism on the following Easter. He would just have time to prepare his soul; so suddenly and finally he adopted an ascetic rule of life. He had the African taste for paroxysm, and he had never been a man for half measures of any kind. He renounced Satan, his works and his pomps, and in this he knew what he was doing. With great care he prepared himself to be worthy of receiving what he had expected from baptism—namely, exalting faith and certitude.

"Too late have I loved You, O Beauty so ancient and so new, too late have I loved You! Behold You were within me, while I was outside: it was there that I sought You, and, a deformed creature, rushed headlong upon those things of beauty which You have made. You were with me, but I was not with You. They kept me far from You, those fair things which, if they were not in You, would not exist at all.

"You have called to me and have cried out and have shattered my deafness. You have blazed forth with light, and have shone upon me, and You have put my blindness to flight! . . . I have tasted You, and I hunger and thirst after You. You have touched me and I have burned for Your peace.

"When I shall cleave to You with all my being, no more will there be pain and toil for me. . . . Where did I find you that I might learn to know You? You were not in my memory before I learned to know You. Where then have I found You, if not in Yourself and above me? There is no place, both backward do we go and forward, and there is no place. Everywhere, O Truth, You give hearing to all who consult You."

At the same time Alypius was preparing himself for baptism. He valiantly attempted to bring his body into subjection by the hardest of physical trials, even to the point of walking with bare feet on the icy winter ground.

They went to Milan and during this stay Augustine wrote his work *On the Immortality of the Soul* as a complement to *The Soliloquies.*

"Cease thy groans, for the human soul is immortal."

"The soul, which is superior to matter, should be treated no less well than matter. Now matter, infinitely divisible, cannot be reduced to nothingness."

"No man can create himself."

Their second stay in Milan was troubled by political upheavals. The usurper Maximus had finally fought his way into Italy; Valentinian, his mother and sisters had fled to Thessalonica by sea. The pagan general Merobaudius had committed suicide. The Emperor Theodosius in the beginning saw these tragic events as a punishment for Valentinian's and Justina's attachment to the Arian heresy. But the first Augustus soon took alarm when he saw Maximus successful in rallying to himself the African provinces with the support of the cruel dictator Gildo. After many delays Theodosius advanced to the attack, and the first battle took place at the river Sava. Maximus' forces were defeated by Theodosius' army, which was composed mainly of barbarian troops.

On April 24, 387, the Saturday night before Easter Sunday, Augustine and Alypius received baptism from the hands of Ambrose. Adeodatus and Navigius were baptized at the same time.

After their baptism, Augustine and Alypius had no other thought than to return to Africa. At the beginning of August they left Milan with Monica, Adeodatus, Evodius and Navigius. Their plan was to go to Ostia and there embark on a ship for Carthage. Augustine wished to resume in Tagaste the cenobitic life he had begun at Cassiciacum, and Monica would arrange to take care of their daily needs. There the Christian philosophers could live in peace, their time wholly devoted to their search for God.

When they crossed the Apennines they found Maximus' bands still occupying the region, which was delivered over to pillage and violence. The journey was dangerous and exhausting, and as they reached Ostia, Monica fell ill.

The tyrant Gildo, Maximus' ally, was attempting to starve Rome into submission. He had cut off the wheat supply and had set up a stringent blockade so that ships could no longer cross the Mediterranean.

Augustine and his companions were therefore forced to remain in Ostia awaiting a ship. Traffic on the Mediterranean, formerly so accessible from Italy, was becoming most uncertain and was so to remain for fourteen hundred years after this time.

The port of Ostia was then a busy one, for it was the warehouse of Rome. During the past three centuries the city had grown in importance, and was modern, elegant and comfortable with its forum, shops, barracks, baths, theaters and galleried thoroughfares paved with large stones.

Augustine and Monica now knew the hour of separation

was at hand. Augustine's conversion and baptism had brought peace to Monica's soul. They had become very close to one another in a union that went far beyond earthly ties.

"She and I stood leaning out from a certain window, where we could look into the garden within the house we had taken at Ostia on the Tiber, where, removed from the crowds, we were resting up after the hardships of a long journey, in preparation for the voyage. We were alone, conversing together most tenderly, 'forgetting those things that are behind, and stretching forth to those that are before.'"

This sublime conversation between mother and son is recorded by Augustine in one of the most celebrated passages of his *Confessions:*

"Our discourse had been brought to the point that the highest delight of fleshly senses, in the brightest corporeal light, when set against the sweetness of that life seemed unworthy not merely of comparison with it, but even of remembrance. Then, raising ourselves up with a more ardent love to the Selfsame, we proceeded step by step through all bodily things up to that heaven whence shine the sun and the moon and the stars down upon the earth. . . .

"And while we discoursed of this and panted after it, we attained to it in a slight degree by the effort of our whole hearts. . . . And we turned back again to the noise of our mouths, where a word both begins and ends. . . . We said: If for any man the tumult of the flesh fell silent, silent the images of earth, and of the waters, and of the air; silent the heavens; silent for him the very soul itself . . . and God alone speaks, not through things but through Himself, so that we hear His Word, not uttered by a tongue of flesh, or by an angel's voice, or by the sound of thunder, or by the riddle of a similitude, but by Himself whom we love in these things, Himself we hear without their aid—even as we then reached out and in swift thought attained to that Eternal Wisdom which abides over all things—if this could be prolonged, and other visions of a far inferior kind could be withdrawn, and this one alone ravish, and absorb, and hide away its beholder within its deepest joys, so that sempiternal life might be such as was that moment of understanding for which we sighed— would this not be: 'Enter into the joy of your Lord?' "

As night fell, Monica sighed and ended the conversation with these gentle words:

"Son, for my own part, I now find no delight in anything in this life. What I can still do here, and why I am here, I do not know, now that all my hopes in this world have been accomplished. One thing there was, for which I desired to linger a little while in this life, that I might see you a Catholic Christian before I died. God has granted this to me in more than abundance, for I see you His servant, with even earthly happiness held in contempt. What am I doing here?"

She had earned rest.

"What I said to her in answer to this," Augustine adds, "I do not entirely recall, for scarcely five days later, or not much more, she fell sick of fever."

She was weak and painfully thin. Her black eyes glowed feverishly in her dark face, which was furrowed by deep wrinkles. One day she lost consciousness. Everyone rushed to her and she soon recovered her senses. Seeing Augustine and Navigius standing beside her bed, she said in the manner of someone seeking something: "Where was I?"

They could not hide their anxiety. But finally she smiled and managed to say:

"Here you will bury your mother."

Augustine did not speak. Trying to keep back his tears, he turned nervously aside, unable to hide his grief. But Navigius asked Monica if it would not be better to die and be laid to rest in her own country. She made a great effort to listen to his words, then gazed at him reproachfully, because he was concerned about such things. Turning to Augustine, who had succeeded in mastering his emotion, she said almost in anger:

"See what he says! Put this body away anywhere. Don't let care about it disturb you. I ask only this of you, that you remember me at the altar of the Lord, wherever you may be."

On the ninth day of her sickness death came gently and silently. When Augustine saw that she had breathed her last, he closed her eyes. The boy Adeodatus burst into sobs.

Augustine bade his son to master his grief. Monica, he told him, had not looked on death as something evil; rather she had regarded it as a reward. Now it was the task of Augustine and those close to him to merit such a reward themselves. Still Adeodatus found it hard to stop his tears, for he deeply loved his good grandmother despite her severity.

Evodius, however, began to sing the Psalm: "I will sing of mercy and judgment unto You, O Lord." All present joined in with him.

Monica's body was carried to the church in Ostia, and Augustine accompanied it. During the Mass of requiem he shed no tear, nor even during the prayers said beside the grave. He had vowed this to himself, thinking that since death is not sad for those who depart, it should be a cause of rejoicing for those they leave behind.

Even so, his heart was crushed with sorrow. To store up in his memory he had only a few days of complete communion with a mother against whom he had struggled so long, a mother he had caused so much sorrow and so many tears. All that day he was further distressed by the sadness he saw in the eyes of those about him, and he implored the Lord to deliver him from his own humiliating state of weakness. Mechanically he went to the baths, and he came out as wretched as when he went in, feeling as though he were separated from himself—as though his own soul had left him when Monica died. When night came he was worn out with fatigue and was able to sleep. On awaking he found the violence of his grief had abated, and that at last he could weep before God, over her and for her. His pent-up tears flowed freely and finally his sorrow was eased.

"I took joy from her testimony, when in that last illness she mingled her endearments with my good deeds and called me 'her good son.' With great love and affection she recalled that she had never heard me speak a harsh or disrespectful word to her. Yet, O my God who made us, what comparison was there between the honor she had from me and the services that she rendered to me? When I was bereft of such great consolation, my heart was wounded through and my life was as if ripped asunder. For out of her life and mine one life had been made."

Augustine, his brother, his son, and his friends wandered disconsolately about Ostia. Still the boats from Africa failed to arrive. It seemed apparent there would be no delivery whatever of wheat—either for trade or tax purposes—before the Mediterranean was closed for the winter.

Augustine decided to remain no longer in this port, for all activity had stopped, the inhabitants were reduced to poverty and famine loomed. He had no money left and Ostia offered no means of earning a livelihood.

Should he go to Rome? And if he did, could he avoid his former friends among the Manichaeans and the philosophers? However, Rome was the reasonable solution, for there he could get in touch with Catholic communities, study their rules and find models for the group he expected to establish in Tagaste. Also he would find pupils and could earn his living.

The four men and the youth set out, since this was Augustine's decision. The frail little man was their undisputed leader, and what he decided always seemed best to them.

Augustine no longer wore his African garb. He had clothed himself in the black robe of the Eastern monks, with a cowl and leather belt. This was henceforth to be his dress and he was never to wear any other.

During that winter many political and military events transpired. Theodosius crossed the Julian Alps; Maximus was made prisoner and massacred by the soldiers. In Africa, Gildo submitted to Rome without a struggle. Properly speaking, he was under the jurisdiction of the conqueror, and the wind was blowing from Rome. He would wait a little while before starting another rebellion.

Augustine directed his small community and gave lessons, covering Rome in every direction as he had done several years previously. He also undertook to write a book on the Manichaeans. This was his way of uprooting the last blade of this noxious weed from his heart and his thought. He wrote as though locked in battle with the heresy.

Returning from exile in Thessalonica, the Emperor Valentinian organized on the coast of Sicily a punitive expedition against his enemies. But his mother Justina died and Theodosius took advantage of this to remain in Italy and send the young emperor to battle in Gaul.

Peace on the Mediterranean was restored, and Gildo increased his shipments of wheat as proof of his loyalty to Theodosius. Augustine and his company were at last able to find a ship to carry them to Carthage.

Augustine disembarked in that same port of Carthage where one morning he had left his mother overcome by such deep grief. He trod the streets of a city where only a few years before he had shown himself insolent, proud, and cocksure. Now it was a new man who followed the shadow of his former self.

By chance he met one of his students, Eulogius, who had become a teacher in Carthage. The latter told him that one evening as he was leafing through a volume of Cicero, the subject of his lesson for the day following, he had been unable to understand an obscure passage. That night Eulogius had seen his old teacher Augustine appear at his bedside and heard him explain clearly the passage of Cicero which so perplexed him.

"It was not I," Augustine protested, "and it would not have been my wish to do so. At that time I was asleep or doing something quite other. In any case, I was certainly not thinking of Eulogius or of Cicero."

Augustine still owned on the outskirts of Tagaste the farm

he had inherited from his father. He decided to live there
and try to re-create the same atmosphere as at Cassiciacum.
He sold several fields and distributed the proceeds to the
poor; then he made over his farm with its dependencies to
the Catholic community of Tagaste on the condition it might
be used by himself and his disciples. Thus Patricius' farm
was transformed into a sort of lay community where Augustine resided with Alypius, Evodius and Adeodatus. Soon
this first core was joined by other disciples.

Their rule was limited to prayer and meditation in common. Otherwise each was free to come and go as he pleased.

Augustine immediately set to work, writing or dictating to
others. He finished his book *On the Morals of the Catholic
Church* and the study on the Manichaeans he had begun in
Rome. He dictated a treatise *On the Soul* in the form of a
dialogue with Evodius. Finally he wrote *On Eighty-three
Different Questions* in which he gave his opinion on numerous theological and moral problems, applying to Christian
doctrine the Socratic method of discussing a subject with oneself with the help of stimulation given from time to time by
the presence and questions of attentive listeners.[1]

To rid himself of the last shadows of Manichaeism which
sometimes haunted him, Augustine undertook to draw a contrast between Catholic and Manichaean thought. "It is because there is evil in the world that one believes in God; it is
the existence of this same evil that causes one to doubt in
Him." The first book, *On the Morals of the Catholic Church*
is divided into thirty-three chapters. The second book was to
be *On the Morals of the Manichaeans*.

In a storm of polemical and pitiless words Augustine attacked with vigor, humor, anger, violence and irony. He knew
his friends of other days; he sought, he said, to cure and not
to distress them; nevertheless it was first necessary to talk to
them straight from the shoulder.

"The Gospel forbids us to throw holy things to dogs. Do
not be offended if I speak to you in this way. In other days

I myself barked; I was one of those dogs of which the Gospels speak. Then I was treated as I deserved, since instead of being given the bread of instruction, I was made to feel the lash of the whip.

"Ah, how quickly you will be disabused of these ideas if you will but seek out in the Catholic Church those best instructed in sacred doctrine and will listen to them as I listened to you for the nine years you kept me in error and played with my credulity."

He then began a long panegyric of the Catholic Church "which knows how to form men by instructions and exercises proportioned to the strength and age of each one, which in its salutary teachings has foreseen and understood everything.

"What is the reason that we do evil things?

"Not being able to solve this problem, I was so troubled that if in my case the passion for truth had not brought God's help to my aid, I should never have escaped.

"Who created me? God who is Goodness itself. Then why did there arise in me the will to do evil and not to do good?

"Did God plant in me this bitter germ? From whence came evil into the world? If He could have prevented it, why did God not do so?

"This is the major question. We are steeped in anguish and anger. The animals form a society better than the society of men. Nevertheless, every being at first is good; we call a corrupted nature bad.

"For the Manichaeans, Evil is a substance. If Evil exists, we must admit the existence of an evil principle. Evil, say the Manichaeans, is that which is *contrary to the nature of things*. I reply: Being has no contrary save Nonbeing. There is no nature which is contrary to God. Evil is not a being; it can only be the privation of Good. There can be no privation of anything except of what exists."

More than ever Augustine wished to be a teacher and a leader. But no longer would he instruct his pupils in vain eloquence; rather he would lead them on the road to Truth.

"Without brusquely cutting off young men from sensible ideas and worldly letters, from which it is difficult not to be attached, I try by lessons in reasoning to turn them away little by little and, through love of unchanging Truth, to attach them to God, sole master of all things. If I myself frequented poets and grammarians, this was forced on me by the necessities of the voyage I made."

Isolated from the world, separated from most of his friends, he began a voluminous correspondence. He was consulted from every quarter, and from all sides questions were asked of him. These questions he would propound to himself; in answering them he dissipated his own anxiety, fortified his knowledge and constructed his stronghold. He was like the guardian of a lighthouse attacked all about by the fury of the sea; he must shore up the breaches in the wall and at the same time give light to vessels that were in danger. This was his work—to use his vast intellect, his tremendous power of dialectic, as a fencer uses his sword, to deliver to his adversary the blow that cannot be parried.

He answered all letters that came to him on a staggering variety of spiritual matters. For example, Nebridius asked him questions of this kind:

"Can memory work without imagination?"

"How do devils inspire men with dreams and illusions at night?"

"Why was the Son made flesh rather than the Father?"

"Does supreme and eternal Wisdom include within itself the idea of each individual man?"

Augustine replied with inexhaustible patience, discussing, explaining, enlarging, sometimes carried away by his prodigious facility to the point that his letter became a book.

Nebridius asked him to come to Carthage where he was teaching, but Augustine refused. On the other hand, he begged his friend to join him in the retreat at Tagaste. Nebridius replied that he was ill. Augustine wondered if he should visit him but he could neither take his companions with him nor leave them behind. Should he travel back and forth, staying sometimes with Nebridius and sometimes with them? The trip from Tagaste to the outskirts of Carthage was hard; he would have neither leisure nor repose. Moreover, Augustine was not well himself and could not do everything he would have liked. "So in this case," he concluded, "one must resign oneself not to wish what cannot be done."

Augustine's letters filled Nebridius with delight. "They are unparalleled," he said. "I do not mean in length but in the importance of the matters discussed. At times I think I hear Plato speaking, at others Plotinus, and sometimes Jesus Christ Himself."

Augustine wrote his book *On the Teacher* for his son Adeodatus. The father answers the questions of his son whose mental depth sometimes "frightens him." Adeodatus was sixteen years old and his precocious gifts are revealed in the questions he places before his father who dedicated to him his translation of Aristotle's *Categories*.

On the Teacher is also conceived along Socratic lines, containing Adeodatus' questions and Augustine's replies. This work is of particular interest in that it sets forth Augustine's position regarding the culture of antiquity and the culture of Christianity. In its course Adeodatus is instructed in the principles of the logic of concept, that is to say, in the dialectical discipline so important in Augustine's eyes.

He wished to inject a philosophical turn into grammar itself. For example, one of Vergil's poems is being explained to a child. The pupil is first asked to give the sense of each of the words. Then Augustine would have him reflect on the explanation itself: to explain *one word* he has had to make use of *other words*. Thus he passes from the notion of a sign to the thing signified: "Despite appearances, can it be said that our knowledge is increased by words, by signs? Let us put aside material realities in advance; what remains are *ideas*. These can be communicated only by signs, but must not the hearer already comprehend their meaning if these signs are to be understood? Thus words can only *prompt our attention* and invite us to listen to the teacher *within ourselves*. Now this teacher is Christ.

"How can we perceive harmony in physical objects and be certain that it exists if our mind does not perceive a perfect harmony? Knowledge is light and seeing is synonymous with knowing. Truth is perceived by the light of the intellect. To see God is to seize the very essence of the divine, but it is impossible to see God without first bringing about by our own efforts a deep transformation in our lives."

Adeodatus was to die two years later at the age of eighteen. Nebridius became a Christian and followed him shortly afterward.

Augustine wrote to Romanianus, to Paulinus of Nola, to people in Africa and Italy whom he had never met. He wrote so much he grew short of paper and asked for tablets from Romanianus who once more prospered in Carthage, since Gildo feared to trouble him just then. Augustine also helped his fellow citizens with their affairs; the good people of Tagaste were proud of him and came to him at all hours to ask for advice.

With all this, he still had time to study the Scriptures, to brush up his knowledge of Greek, and to write six books *On Music*. This work has as its aim to guide those who love literature and poetry to God. He recommends music as a means of rising to the very borders of the Infinite.

"What exquisite modulations fill the air when the nightingale pours forth his song. . . . His voice, so full, melodious and sweet, seems as the very song of spring."

De Musica was to be composed of twelve books, but Augustine finished only six of them. Why did he write this work? He addressed it to "the cultured men of a decadent age" who had grown weary of rhetoric and had no great enthusiasm for metaphysical studies, but who were interested in the "liberal arts." He wished to attract them by writing of what interested them in order to lead them to higher things.

De Musica is made up of five books on pure metrics, and ends with a philosophical essay. For Augustine music was a mathematical science like arithmetic or geometry. Nevertheless he "experienced" music in the modern sense of the word and responded to it with intense delight. The liturgical songs, he said, had a powerful attraction for him, and he never forgot the hours at Milan when Ambrose was there. This was "earthly food" of a very high order to him.

Nevertheless, what Augustine has to say in his work on music is something quite different, for he deals with it in a purely scientific way. The singing bird is not *skilled* in the liberal art of music, and those who react to music in an instinctive way are excluded from the debate.[2] Augustine begins with rhythm and numerical elements; then little by little philosophical problems are introduced—nothing less is dealt with than the relationship of the body to the soul.[3] The book ends as the philosopher and the theologian grow silent to make place for the mystic's prayer.

Of True Religion was the last of the works written during this period at Tagaste. Augustine sent it to Carthage to his dear Romanianus who "having left the errors of the Manichaeans, had not yet embraced the Catholic faith, and he hoped to convert him."

"I have written those things on the Catholic religion," he told Romanianus, "which it has pleased God to put into my mind. I plan to send it to you before going to see you, provided I do not run out of paper. Be so kind as to excuse the writing which has been done hurriedly by those who are with me."

Augustine exhorts men to embark on an eager search for truth. The least of men should adore Him who is worshiped by the highest among the angels. And he concludes: "Our ancestors were drawn to the Christian faith by miracles that took place before their eyes, but after the Church was founded

on earth, do we have need of further proof of the divinity of
Jesus Christ?"

When he had finished reading his friend's book, Romanianus became a Christian. He felt he must take this step
after reading such passages as these:

"Men have free will . . . and it is by the will that sin is
committed. . . . God judged that men would serve him better if they served him freely. . . . The angels serve God
freely, and that is to their advantage, not God's. God needs
no good things from others, for all good comes from Himself. . . .

"Even in this corruptible body it is permitted to us to work
toward righteousness, to lay aside all pride and submit to God
alone, not to trust in ourselves but to commit ourselves to
be ruled and defended by Him alone. So with God's guidance
a man of goodwill can turn in the midst of the troubles of
this present life to the practice of virtue and courage."

Coming to the Incarnation of the Word, Augustine described it "as the greatest lovingkindness God had shown in
His dealings with the human race."

"When His only Son, coeternal and cosubstantial with the
Father, deigned to assume human nature, He showed . . .
how lofty a place among creatures belonged to human nature, in that He appeared to men not merely visibly—for He
could have done that in some ethereal body adapted to our
weak powers of vision—but as a true man. The assuming of
our nature was to be also its liberation. He honored all humanity when He became a man born of woman.

"He did nothing by violence, but everything by persuasion.
. . . By His miracles He, being God, produced faith in God,
and by His Passion, endured in the human nature He had
assumed, He furthered respect for that human nature. . . .

"When, as God, He was about to turn water into wine, He
said to His mother: 'Woman, depart from me; what have I to
do with thee? My hour is not yet come.' Yet when His hour
had come when, as man, He should die, He recognized this

same mother from the cross and commended her to the disciple whom He loved more than the others. . . .

"The primal vice of the rational soul is to do what the highest truth forbids. Thus man was driven from paradise into the present world, that is to say, from eternal things to temporal, from abundance to poverty, from strength to weakness. Not, however, from substantial good to substantial evil; but from eternal good to temporal good, from spiritual to carnal good, from intelligible to sensible good, from the highest to the lowest good. There is therefore a good to which it is sin for the rational soul to attach itself because it belongs to a lower order of being."

Augustine's stern and ringing words in this book not only brought Romanianus to a decision, but led to a wave of conversions throughout Africa.

Each spring Augustine was present at the baptisms in the church at Tagaste. On those mornings the catechumens emerged one by one from the robing room and, descending the steps of the pool, entered the water up to their waists. Then the priest would pour from a shell the baptismal water upon their heads. Returning to the robing room, the new Christians clothed themselves in their white woolen garments and formed a procession to proceed into the nave of the church.

Augustine went every morning to the Tagaste church, approaching it up a wide avenue paved with stones polished by the going and coming of many feet. Always he found this thoroughfare filled with a motley crowd—Negroes from the palm groves, shepherds down from the high plateaus, mules, little Numidian horses, camels carrying heavy, swaying tents covered with multicolored awnings. Hawkers offered passersby pomegranates, dried figs and cakes dripping with honey. Arriving in the atrium of the church "where chandeliers with colored prisms cast their glow on the walls and columns of Numidian marble," and where the mosaics behind the altar scintillated in the light, Augustine would pray and meditate.

The cenobitic life he led with his disciples satisfied him completely. He had arranged for discipline to be left more and more to the judgment of each. He found real appeasement in his intellectual labors and perpetual quest for God, despite his attacks of asthma, his nocturnal fevers, his insomnia and the sharp anxieties that flashed through his mind and obliged him to rush to his writing table to pen a refutation of this error or that. Would he be able to finish out his life in this community of laymen? It seemed probable to him, and he wished for nothing else than to recapture those moments of grace he had known on the balcony at Ostia with Monica, his mother.

But this was not to be.

The situation of the Catholic Church in North Africa entered a critical phase toward the end of the year 390. Supported by the tyrant Gildo, the Donatist schism had spread like wildfire; the number of Circumcellions, highwaymen and murderers had increased, and they had been emboldened by the weakness and hesitation of the Catholic metropolitan.

Valerius, the bishop of Hippo, wrote Augustine asking him to visit him; he would like to discuss with him his latest book. At the same time Augustine was asked by an inhabitant of Hippo for his spiritual help, and so despite his uncertain health and love for work and solitude, Augustine set out. It was against the grain, for perceiving his popularity among his coreligionists, he had hitherto been careful not to leave his refuge.

There was at this time a great shortage of priests, and Valerius, the bishop of Hippo, a Greek by birth, did not know the Punic language. This made very difficult his task as administrator, judge, confessor and worker among the poor, and particularly was he hindered in his preaching.

Hippo was a prosperous port city, extending toward the plain and spread out over two hills. One of these hills faced the sea and was dominated by the Basilica of Peace; a fortress crowned the other. The city had two rivers, and one, which made a complete circle around it before casting itself into the sea, was crossed by a bridge with eleven arches. The other river, the Sebous, flowed into Hippo from the plains to the south, and on this was built an inner, artificial port, very large and embanked by a great wharf.

Facing away from the sea, one saw hills to the northeast, and to the southeast dunes continuing all the way to Carthage. Directly behind the city were oak trees as far as the eye could reach, and an aqueduct which brought to Hippo the waters of the Aurès.[4]

On the day of his arrival (at the beginning of the year 391) Augustine went at once to the basilica. At that very moment Bishop Valerius was in the pulpit bewailing the lack of priests. His pleas aroused no response. Mixed in with the congregation, Augustine was listening when suddenly those around him pointed him out, saying, "It is Augustine, the sage of Tagaste, the wise and pious Augustine!"

He was immediately surrounded by a great crowd, which pushed and dragged him before the bishop, as the cries grew louder and louder.

All he could hear was: "Augustine—a priest!"

Augustine tried to free himself, to escape, to flee, but he could not. In those days when the Christian people designated a worthy man to the bishop, the prelate had to make the man a priest. It was a custom that could not be broken.

The crowd about Augustine became threatening; he had to climb two steps of the pulpit in order not to be smothered. The bishop freed him, and tried to lead him away, but the crowd grew denser and demanded a reply.

Augustine's head was filled with a turmoil of contradictory thoughts. Must he leave his hermitage, his studies, his work on the writings of the Fathers of the Church, so often distorted in their translations from the Greek? He could not resign himself to this and sincerely believed it was more useful for him to lead a life of meditation than a life of action.

But it was dangerous to resist the enthusiasm of the faithful, the bishop said. He knew Augustine and recognized his worth—and, who can tell, he might have laid this trap for him himself.

Augustine resigned himself there and then. Once more a great clamor of enthusiasm filled the church.

"Augustine, a priest!" the people cried.

There was nothing for him to do but prepare himself for ordination. "This glowing light which sought the shadow of solitude, was thrust upon the candlestick," Possidius, Augustine's biographer, was later to write.

He was thirty-six years of age, and was to live in Hippo for nearly forty years.

Chapter Seven

THE BISHOP OF HIPPO
391–396

He had never wished to be a priest. Perhaps because he had been a Manichaean he considered he was not worthy. Had he thought of becoming one, the heavy daily duties of this vocation would have deterred him. In his solitude at Tagaste, immersed in his work, he felt inspired and confident he had chosen the right path in his journey toward God. He shrank at the thought of the earthly cares with which a priest is burdened—he would have to deal with ecclesiastical affairs, perhaps even to preach. A former orator who had gained his rhetorical knowledge in the world, he did not want to fall back into a role he had renounced forever.

He wished to return to his home, and wrote Valerius asking for a delay in order to recover "self-mastery" and to "prepare" himself. The tone of his letter was sad, for nothing came easily to him, and he always foresaw the problems and difficulties in any task he undertook. Valerius consented for him to make a retreat, but specified he must remain in the neighborhood of Hippo.

Augustine wrote to Tagaste requesting his companions to join him; since he must obey, he intended to be obeyed. Hastily he prepared for them a temporary dwelling, and in this new retreat he planned for them to follow a rule of life similar to the one they had adopted at Tagaste and at Cassiciacum. When they joined him, all went on living as before. Augustine listened attentively to the spiritual reading and arranged for discussions to be held at mealtime. He had these words inscribed on the wall of the refectory: "He who speaks ill of the absent is not worthy to sit at this table."

In the monastery which they built for themselves, Alypius, Evodius, Severus, Possidius and "other servants of God" led a community life according to the rule "established by the holy Apostles." No one owned anything himself and to each was given those things he needed. Augustine was now in a way the "superior" of a monastic group. This was the first step.

The day of his ordination soon came. His mind was greatly troubled, for he was thinking of Monica and what her joy would have been had she lived. At the moment he was anointed and received the priestly powers, Augustine burst into tears.

Thinking he wept from bitterness because he had not at once received higher ecclesiastical honors than the priesthood, the faithful cried out:

"You are right, Augustine! You should be a bishop!"

Immediately after his ordination, Valerius asked him to preach in his stead. When this was known, protests were made by various of the African bishops. It was not customary, they said; only a bishop had the right to preach. Valerius paid no attention to them, and thanked God he had a "man so capable" to second him.

Old and ill, Valerius often asked the new priest to help him with other tasks. Augustine was not one to show himself unwilling, and little by little the bishop turned over all his duties to him. Augustine heard confessions, instructed the catechumens, went begging for the needs of the poor, managed the property of the diocese—and preached constantly from the first time he mounted the pulpit at the beginning of the year 392.

At the same time he thought he should take up his battle

against the Manichaeans, "the followers of Lucifer." And he wrote *On the Value of Believing*.

Should man be deprived of religion if he could not reach to God through reason? No, it could not be. Learned men should therefore begin by walking in the common road, the safest of all.

"What would remain if we wish to believe only what we understand? It was by faith and not by reason that Jesus instructed the people. Authority was established by his miracles, faith was born of his authority.

"Why did he not perform more miracles? Miracles would cease to attract attention if they were too often repeated. The succession of days and nights, the cycle of the seasons, the falling of the leaves from the trees and their rebirth in spring, the beauty of light, the tones and variety of sounds and sweet smells—all these miracles would overpower one who perceived them for the first time. Yet because we have become accustomed to these prodigies we have become indifferent to them."

Augustine was begged to undertake a public debate with Fortunatus, a famous Manichaean teacher, and he accepted immediately. Fortunatus shrank from the discussion, but there was no escape. The day and place was fixed—the Baths of Sosius—and "notaries" were appointed to take down the debate verbatim. On August 28, 392, a crowd of curious onlookers filled the place where the theological combat was held, and it continued for two whole days.

The Manichaean teacher could not withstand the pitiless questions or the subtle and unanswerable arguments of his opponent. Saying that he would refer the knotty problems to his superiors, he fled Hippo, never to return.

Augustine's first letter *Against the Donatists* dates from the same year. It was addressed to Maximus, the Donatist bishop of Sinitum, a town on the road between Hippo and Carthage. Augustine reproached Maximus for rebaptizing a Catholic deacon and appealed to his religious sense, begging him to place Truth before all other considerations.

"Before the tribunal of Jesus Christ where each man will be accused by his own conscience and judged by Him who sees into the inner recesses of every heart, of what use are a bishop's throne covered with hangings and raised on a dais at the far end of the church, and processions of nuns advancing to meet him as they sing psalms and canticles?

"The Jews who saw Jesus nailed to the cross of infamy did not dare to divide His robe among them, but Christians who know He is seated at the right hand of God dare to dishonor His sacrament."

Augustine's first writing against the Donatists was a psalm in prose made up of as many stanzas as there are letters in the alphabet from A to V, each stanza composed of twelve verses. This alphabetical psalm, which was meant to be sung, contains a summary of the history of Donatism and the reasons the faithful should be on their guard against the heresy.

The council which opened in Hippo on October 8, 393, in the Basilica of Peace and presided over by Aurelius, the bishop of Carthage, was a solemn occasion for Augustine. He preached before the assembled bishops a discourse "on faith and symbols." This was an explanation of symbols but also a condemnation of Manichaean errors to which he could allow "neither truce nor rest."

Augustine's closest friends became priests like himself. Alypius had to leave him, for he was made bishop of Tagaste. Of all Augustine's friends, Licentius, Romanianus' son, was the only one to remain a pagan. He composed verses and sang the praises of his former teacher, but carnal ties bound him to Milan.

Augustine wrote Licentius urging him to ponder on the transitory nature of worldly things, and reproached him with spending his time working on his poetry when so much disorder reigned in his heart.

The ambitions of the terrible Gildo were unleashed by the death of the Emperor Theodosius in 395; the blockade of the Mediterranean was resumed. Nevertheless Romanianus was trying to get to Italy and Augustine gave him a letter to Licentius in which he counseled his former pupil to repair to Nola, where he would meet Paulinus, the bishop, and "should ask him to show him the way to God."

In that year of 395, Augustine finished a book he had begun in Rome after the death of his mother and which he had worked on in Tagaste. This was the treatise *On Free Will*, in which he again adopted the Socratic form of dialogue with his friend Evodius as interlocutor.

It saddened Augustine to have men doubt the happiness that lies in the possession of truth:

"Some cry out they are happy when they are seduced by the perishable beauty of a woman. Others find joy, when they are thirsty and hungry, in abundant and delicate food. Another proclaims his happiness when he is surrounded by the sweet smells of flowers and perfumes. There are those who rejoice in a beautiful voice or the melody of a musical instrument. Gold and silver, the shining whiteness of a pearl, the bright glow of earthly lights, the stars in the sky, bring great joys to human hearts.

"But when Truth with its splendors comes to shed its light upon our reason we are so gross that we find no happiness in it.

"Now, God alone is the principle of all Good, and therefore Truth has been freely granted to us by God Himself. Evil is the disordered movement of the will, which separates itself from immutable Good to cling to transitory goods. It is a voluntary movement which lies within our own power, and would not exist if we did not will it.

"Man does not sin because God has predestined it, but because God is everywhere and at all times present he sees the sin that man commits. Knowing the future, God cannot be ignorant of acts His creatures will commit through the working of their own wills: *Knowledge* of the future is not *constraint* of the future. In the human order of things, God is not the author of what He foresees."

Farther on, Augustine says: "There is in the misery that follows sin something which contributes to the perfection of the world. When pure men are happy the universe appears to them in its true splendor. The perfection and beauty of the universe continue in existence whether the just are joyful or sinners are miserable."

Thus, as Marrou says, Augustine meditated on the supreme aspects of Truth. The reason is enlightened by Truth to the extent it recognizes that Truth. There is within us something higher than reason, and Augustine leads us to conclude in the existence of a reality so exalted that it cannot be anything else than God. "What is encased in time," he says, "is placed in a certain order. The future seems to succeed to the past only because things perish in order that the beauty of time, which flows like a river, may reach its final perfection."

The old Bishop Valerius watched over Augustine as one would guard a treasure. As a matter of fact, certain neighboring churches were so anxious to have him as their bishop there was danger he might be taken away from Hippo. To avoid this, Valerius decided to consecrate Augustine as soon as he could, and to designate him as his successor. Such a measure was contrary to one of the canons of the Council of Nicaea. Valerius consulted Aurelius, the primate of Carthage, and was assured of that prelate's accord with his plan. He then assembled the bishops of Numidia and solemnly declared to them his desire to make Augustine his coadjutor.

The only bishop to protest this promotion was Megalius, the primate of Numidia. Valerius, he said, had already bestowed on Augustine the right to preach in his presence, which was contrary to custom. Now he wanted to appoint him in advance as his successor to the see of Hippo! Much had already been done for this "priest of recent date," only lately converted and, moreover, a former Manichaean steeped (only God knew to what extent!) in the mysteries of those people.

But Augustine won out against Megalius' ill will. The Donatists, with Gildo's support, became masters of the land and all the forces of the Church had to be united to combat them. Augustine was just such a force, and in the end he was consecrated coadjutor bishop of Hippo by Megalius himself.

Nothing was less in accord with Augustine's character than worldly ambition or taste for power. He had bitterly renounced all temporal "success," and his only hope in this life was to draw nearer to God. To do this it seemed to him that one should be alone and should be free. He envied the solitary life of St. Antony in the desert. Nevertheless, who could say whether meditation might not lead to reverie and reverie to laziness? Action might well save him from "egotism." Finally, his forceful temperament, which was in curious contrast with his fragile health, demanded activity, even to the point of exhaustion. Should he sacrifice a part of his intellectual life? Well, it was good to sacrifice things in which one took pleasure, even when they were pure.

In the end Valerius died, and Augustine succeeded him. He had been consecrated coadjutor bishop to Valerius a short time before Christmas of the year 395. At the beginning of 396, Augustine wrote the news to Paulinus of Nola, who rejoiced over it as "a boon to Christendom."

In his fight for Catholic unity, Augustine was struggling in behalf of the Empire and of civilization. There seems no doubt the theological aspect of the quarrel was a secondary consideration, but the Donatist bishops refused with complete bad faith to discuss the matter at all.

For nearly a hundred years the Circumcellions had waged a relentless warfare against the peaceful population of Africa. Farms owned by Catholics were constantly pillaged and burned, and Christians were kidnapped, tortured, massacred and their bodies desecrated by bands of fanatical robbers supported more or less openly by the Donatists. To these miserable men were joined troops of hysterical women, and together they went about burning down farms and fields of grain ready for harvesting, their war cry nothing other than "Praise be to God!"

Was Donatism the feverish expression of an excessive African nationalism? An African sense of nationality did not exist in Augustine's day any more than it does in our own. Hence Donatism was not a separatist movement, politically organized, but a terrorist movement battening on pillage and money obtained by demands of ransom, all supported by a dissident Church and by Gildo for his own aims. They were fighting for unconditional surrender and the massacre or the flight of Catholics from Africa. It was impossible to come to any terms with them.

Nevertheless Augustine constantly wrote letters to the Donatists. The arguments he used were always the same: "Why do you rebaptize Catholics under the pretext that their priests are traitors, and, as such, unworthy to administer the sacraments? It is Jesus' sacrifice and not the virtue of the priest that gives efficacy to baptism. If it were otherwise, of what use was the Redemption? Through Christ's voluntary death, all men are called to salvation."

The life of a bishop in a city like Hippo was not entirely made up of combat against schism and heresy; far from it. It was a life of hard physical toil. The faithful were placed under the protection of their bishop from every point of view. The ecclesiastical domains had to be supervised, claims for justice to be heard each day at great length—Kabyles and Phoenicians were notoriously long-winded—and large numbers of poor people had to be provided for by him.

An able administrator, Augustine established centers of charity on properties left to the Church. He required all his clergy to renounce their possessions in favor of the community and himself gave them the example of a Christlike poverty. He refused to accept a legacy from a father or a mother who disinherited their children in order to make bequests to the Church—he had no intention of impoverishing orphans. He also refused to engage the Church in a lawsuit against the fiscal authorities by accepting certain inheritances from dubious sources, saying: "I accept only donations from those who are pious and good."

He also refused to allow the practice of forcing the priesthood upon a passing stranger as had happened in his own case.

The diocese owned several large estates or "foundations" where freed slaves, agricultural workers and even artists were housed. These modest people were exempt from taxes and found "the regime of the bishop more paternal than the civil regime."

Augustine had to study every organizational detail, to supervise agents and peasants. For hours he rode about the countryside on his mule visiting vineyards and olive orchards. He had to learn about the quality of grapes and wheat, to understand contracts of every kind. He had to listen to litigants and render decisions, acting as judge in civil suits. Often the opposing parties would follow him into his house or the basilica in order to convince him of the justice of their cause.

There is scarcely need to say he tried more often to reconcile differences than to render justice. From his pulpit he gave wise advice to litigants, but it was not often followed. He had to give audiences daily and on fast days all day long.

Preaching was a no less consuming task. He had to give a sermon every morning and sometimes several times a day. He spoke in a familiar, almost popular language, a mixture of Latin and Punic. Notaries took down his sermons, which he rarely wrote out in advance—this explains the reason that sometimes he began to speak on one subject and ended on another. He was small, thin, stooped and already graying, and had allowed his beard to grow in the manner of the cenobitic monks.

The faithful assisted at Mass standing, the men on one side, the women on the other. The congregation expressed "their emotions and opinions with complete freedom," and were as noisy as spectators at a theater or circus, applauding and sometimes even interrupting the preacher. Augustine loved this tumult and contact with his audience. As he spoke he looked directly into the eyes of his listeners. He occasionally told a robust joke and was not repelled by the smells that emanated from the piled-up crowd of humanity in the church.

"Ah," he cried, "I perceive by the smell that I must have spoken at length today."

He stressed his role as a bishop as little as possible, and was genial, full of good will, and a ready listener. He knew how to touch the emotions of his hearers as well as to convince them. He used images, parables and comparisons that appealed to them and embellished them as the occasion required. For instance, "The perverse Donatists are like asses and horses which kick the people who are trying to cure their ills."

He made constant allusions to little happenings of the day. If there was a crowd at the circus and only a few people in church, he said: "So much the better! This will give my voice a rest."

He said: "My brothers, you like to come to hear me, but what is it you like? If it is I, even that is good because I wish you to love me, but I do not wish to be loved for myself. For my part, I love you in Christ, so in your turn love me in Him. All Christians are the servants of the same Master. If today from the height of this pulpit I give you celestial food, I remember that only a very few years ago I myself received this spiritual nourishment from a very lowly place."

He commented on political events, local matters and on the crimes of the Circumcellions. This took courage, for the Donatists had Gildo's ear, and were trying with his support to detach Africa from the Empire.

Augustine's words flowed easily and he made use of pithy and familiar images. At times the teacher of rhetoric reappeared and he rose to great heights of oratory as when he spoke on one of his favorite themes—God's goodness and the joy to be derived from His teachings.

Of his approach to his listeners he said: "Our arrogance

would indeed be odious if we refuse to allow men who are our brothers to sit by our side—even more is this true of men we are trying to persuade to become our brothers. If an orator perceives that his audience is yawning, he has only to say such things as will bring their attention back.

"To be listened to, the preacher should possess a joy that is calm and deep, the joy of certitude. He should himself show the joy that conviction brings. Even if we are sad, we should remember that Jesus died for those who are listening to us. Should the thought of bringing new disciples to Him not be sufficient reason to restore our own joy?"

We may indeed call Augustine's life a full one. He carried on his apostolic activities, his administrative work, his combat against heresies and schisms, and finally the progressive construction of his theological, philosophical and pedagogical writings. And besides this he traveled, visiting not only different places in his own diocese but others beyond its borders. He was asked to speak in this place and then that. The Catholic Church was being attacked on all sides by heretics and pagans, and needed the tongues of a hundred men to defend it. The Word must be spread everywhere!

Just as the Catholic Church was being attacked on all sides, so the Roman Empire was being subjected to increasing pressures. Valentinian II remained in Gaul, where he met his death by assassination on May 15, 392. Count Arbogast, his murderer and the first Frank to hold a high post in the Empire, without changing his name to a Roman form, then began to act as administrator of the West and as delegate of Theodosius, the first Augustus. He suddenly decided to have Eugenius, a former teacher of rhetoric, proclaimed emperor on August 22, 392. This Eugenius, who owed his high position to the Franks, tried (but in vain) to win the support of Bishop Ambrose of Milan in order to obtain recognition by Theodosius. After a campaign which ravaged the whole of the Frankish country, he concluded a treaty with the Alemanni.

Once again fratricidal war became inevitable, and this time

the offensive was taken by the pagans. It seemed as though the days of Julian had returned. The possessions of the pagan temples were restored, and buildings constructed from materials taken from former temples were demolished. Ambrose had to flee from Milan as the usurper Eugenius made his triumphal entry into that city.

In January 393, Theodosius had raised his son Honorius to the dignity of second Augustus, intending for him to become the ruler of the West. Theodosius proceeded without haste to make preparation for war against Eugenius and against the revival of paganism in the West. He assembled all the mobile forces in the East and especially the barbarians, among them twenty thousand Goths whose chief was Alaric.

The general of Eugenius' troops was Arbogast, who decided to take a defensive position and to wait behind the Julian Alps for Theodosius' attack. On the day of that attack a windstorm arose with frightful violence, and in the great confusion of this battle a part of the Western army was exterminated, and the remaining troops went over to the side of the victor. Eugenius was made prisoner and was assassinated by his own soldiers on September 6, 394. Arbogast committed suicide.

Theodosius, who showed clemency toward his vanquished opponents, delivered an allocution before the Senate in Rome in which he solemnly exhorted the pagan senators to embrace the Christian faith. The law which prohibited paganism in the East was extended to the West, and the number of followers of the gods was reduced to a few Neoplatonists and the members of certain great senatorial families. Paganism no longer played a political role.

During the victory celebration that followed, the Emperor Theodosius died suddenly on January 17, 395. He seems to have had little confidence in the abilities of his eldest son Arcadius, who now became the first Augustus, and in his will had not even made him regent for his younger brother, Honorius. He confided this guardianship to Stilicho, the son of a

Vandal officer who could not wear the purple but whose daughter had married Honorius, the second Augustus.

Alaric and his Goths had again arrived in the Balkan peninsula. When they learned of Theodosius' death, in March 395, they resumed hostilities and laid waste the country, fighting their way to the very walls of Constantinople.

Alaric then entered central Greece, took Athens, burned Corinth and invaded the Peloponnesus without meeting any opposition. For his part, Gildo made a final effort to free Africa from the power of Rome while at the same time he robbed the Africans of their possessions with the help of the Circumcellions. Again he reduced the shipments of grain to Italy, with the result that uprisings broke out in Rome because of famine.

A Christian at thirty-three, a priest at thirty-six, and a bishop at forty-one, Augustine could not change the mental habits formed by his earlier training. At least he did all he could to correct, complete or add to this formation as he drew closer to his Christian ideal.

The result he desired he realized at Hippo, for he was able to unify the different influences that had played a role in his development. At Cassiciacum he had given himself to God, as Marrou says, "with a soul still pagan, still subject to the limitations of worldly knowledge."

His theology was stern because he was a convert. He himself said: "Within the soul of a convert who has been an unbeliever and a sinner there develops a sort of fanatical anxiety. The remembrance of his past errors exasperates him." Augustine's thought was subordinated to one dominant preoccupation—one did not give "a place" to God, one gave everything to Him.

Augustine was a pastor of souls in the most complete sense, refusing no tasks no matter how thankless or painful they might be. This contemplative did not shrink from action in the world and his life was guided by the demands of his ministry.

As a bishop he was mindful of the apostolic responsibilities of his position. He must preserve the faith of the flock entrusted to him and "bring the mind of Christ to his brothers." Money matters, ecclesiastical discipline, religious controversies, interminable debates with the Donatists—all these made heavy demands upon his time, but the results were highly fruitful because they brought him into contact with the daily life of other men. It was in part because of this he insisted that learning should be made subordinate to and incorporated in the Christian faith, and have as its aim the perfection of spiritual life, the one and necessary thing.

"All the moral teaching of Augustine," writes Marrou, "is contained in the mental distinction between 'enjoying' and 'using,' *frui* and *uti*: in God alone, the Supreme Being and our End, is it lawful to rest and have joy; all the rest we should only use as instruments, as means subordinate to this end. . . . Augustine will allow no delay to define the subordinate ends; he will only call them means. Travelers on our way to our happy fatherland, we have no right to linger, enjoying the beauty of the country we pass through, or the charm of the journey."

According to Augustine, classical literature was shot through with paganism and seemed inseparable from the worship of idols. It was immoral in its exaltation of sensuality and a source of heresy and irreligion. One should no longer dwell on how to say or write things well, but rather on the core of what is to be said and not the form in which the words are expressed.

Language is a method that permits us to communicate our thoughts, but it merits no attention "in itself." This sacred orator narrowly missed denouncing eloquence, for he was trying to put away the thought of everything that separates us from God. According to him, we should also consider as childish distractions the study of such things as the behavior of a lizard or the astronomers' precise calculation of the movements of the stars. Even if they were true additions to knowledge, such things had no bearing on salvation. "Happy is he who knows You, even if he does not know such things. Indeed, a man who knows both You and these things too is not the happier because of them," Augustine says in his *Confessions*.

As Marrou says, "With Augustine, learning was subordinated to the religious life because of the spirit which completely animated him. Study should be a second consideration to the progress of the soul. Indeed one could spend one's life examining the miracles of nature, the manifestation of the Lord, and still remain a monster of iniquity if one is seeking knowledge and not holiness.

"We too often tend to regard Augustine's teaching from a modern viewpoint. We measure the obscurantist factor in his utilitarian pessimism and think what obstacles it might have placed in the way of the finest discoveries made by the human mind between Augustine's age and our own. But let us place ourselves in the decadent civilization in which he lived, and we cannot fail to see deeply human reasons for his savage revolt against the culture of his time."

Certainly he was neither the first nor the last to seek God and salvation to the exclusion of all else. But before his time the Fathers of the Church had never considered themselves apart from the classical culture. Augustine wrote as "a scholar of the decadence," and he realized the meaning of that decadence. The civilization of antiquity had come to its end, and certain materials had to be saved in order to reconstruct everything on a new plan.

"The knowledge of things divine," he wrote in *De Trinitate*, "is perfectly called wisdom, and that of things human is properly given the name of knowledge; . . . not indeed so as to attribute to this knowledge everything that can be done by man about human things, wherein there is much of empty vanity and mischievous curiosity, but only those things by

which that most health-giving faith which leads to true bless-
edness is begotten, nourished, defended and strengthened. But
in this knowledge most of the faithful are not strong, however strong they may be in the faith itself. For it is one thing
to know only what man *ought* to believe in order to attain to
eternal life, but another to know *in what way* this belief may
both help the pious and be maintained against the impious."

What were to be the bases of the new Christian culture?
Augustine wrote in a letter to Dioscorus, a Christian philosopher who lived in accordance with the Augustinian rule and
at the same time was an avid reader of Plato and Plotinus:

"A Christian may be ignorant of Plato's name, yet he knows
that the philosophers professed to study wisdom. But the
Christian must be on his guard against those who based everything on worldly elements and not on God. However, in
order that they may not consider all philosophers as alike, let
them hear the voice of the Apostle: 'That which is known
of God is manifest to them, for God has manifested it to
them. For the invisible things of Him, from the creation of
the world, are clearly seen, being understood by the things
that are made.'

"But it may also be said that they have not served God as
they should because they have rendered divine honors to other
things, honors which are due to Him alone.

"A Christian who is not versed in philosophy does not use
in his discussions terms of which he is ignorant; he does not
follow the Latins in calling *natural* and the Greeks in calling
physical that part of philosophy which treats of natural things;
or *rational philosophy* or *logic* that part in which rules are
given for distinguishing between what is true and what is
false; or *moral* or *ethical* that part of philosophy which deals
with morality and sovereign Good. Is this to say that such a
Christian does not know that he derives his nature from the
God in whose image he is created?

"The doctrine by which we know Him and know ourselves is that Grace which unites us to Him and to His beatitude."

For Augustine wisdom is the knowledge of God and above all *certitude*. This ideal is difficult to attain on earth and is given to only a very few souls. Wisdom is a search, the compass and method of which are philosophical. "It is by means of dialectics that little by little we come to know and perceive the manifestation of God, and see what most resembles Him in creatures, in man, in the soul, and in reason." This for Augustine was to attain to the highest knowledge of God that man could hope for here below.

For him two attitudes were possible—that of the philosopher and that of the man of simple faith. The first was the attitude of one who seeks knowledge through reason. The second was personified for Augustine by his mother, Monica, and it was because of her that he came to appreciate its value.

He had not yet proclaimed the great importance of prayer or written of grace. Nevertheless in his treatise *On Christian Doctrine* he wrote on the subject of that interior purification "which permits the soul to enter into touch with Wisdom." This was brought about by devotion, divine worship, and participation in the life of the Church which are required of all the faithful no matter what may be the degree of their intellectual attainments.

"Of everyone is required," Marrou notes, "the same complete and sincere belief in the Creed. But of the intellectual more is demanded. He who wishes to grasp the content of the faith must go back to the sources, to Holy Scripture—everything is contained in the Scriptures."

Chapter Eight

THE FATHER OF
CHRISTIAN CULTURE
396–410

Augustine was the insignificant bishop of a poor African diocese and could look forward to no advancement. Stories of his past were repeated behind his back and his earlier Manichaeism was held against him. There were some who distrusted him and his name did not appear on the list of those to receive promotion. He wrote kinds of works and his trenchant and hard-hitting pen made people fear him.

A tireless worker, he corrected his manuscripts, supervised the copyists, and concerned himself with the troubles of the members of his flock, speaking to each in his own language. He could be sharp or genial in turn, blunt in his manner or sympathetic. One had to do what he wanted in order to remain in his favor. He had only one aim—to bring souls to Christ. "We speak," he said, "God teaches us."

He was ill, suffering especially from hemorrhoids. He could, he said, neither walk, sit down or stand up. His asthma caused him nights of insomnia, and sometimes he thought he would die of strangulation; but when daybreak came, he was still alive. His fragile life seemed to hang only on a thread, but that thread was strong.

His clothing was shabby, his tastes modest, and his table frugal. He never wished to buy property, lands or farms for his bishopric. The only use he made of monies given him by the communities of the faithful was to have a hospital built by Leporius. He required his priests to live in community and to put donations given to them individually into the common purse. This was one of the laws of the Augustinian rule.

Twenty-four hours in a day were not enough for all he had to do, and he slept but little. He knew that, faced with pressure from the barbarians, the unity of the Church was absolutely essential. More than ever the Church was suffering from the attacks of the Donatists who, supported by the Circumcellions, forcibly ousted the Catholics from their churches. They rebaptized them and "purified" the basilicas by flooding them with water, after demolishing the altars and throwing salt on the ground they had occupied. They pretended to consider Catholics as damned.

The Circumcellions burned out the eyes of those who resisted them with chalk steeped in vinegar. The Numidian bishop Maximianus almost died under their tortures. The altar of his basilica was overthrown, and his tormentors dragged his bleeding body in the dust. Twice he escaped death, first because the dust staunched his flow of blood, the second because, when thrown from the top of a tower, he fell into a pile of dung. Escaping from his would-be executioners, he fled to Milan to beg justice from the Emperor Honorius.

A priest of the diocese of Hippo, by name Restitutus, a former Donatist, was the victim of horrible attacks. Beaten, besmeared and dressed grotesquely, he was walked up and down before a crowd of jeering onlookers.

Blood flowed daily in the towns and in the countryside, Virgins and even married women were violated. "Cursed are we!" wrote Saint Jerome. "We have become displeasing to God."

The capital of the Donatists was Hippo itself, and soon they were more numerous than the Catholics. They possessed a great basilica where they gave magnificent banquets. From the Basilica Leontiana close by, the Catholics could hear the sounds of these pagan festivities and the orgies with which they ended.

To each of Augustine's attempts to deal with them, the Donatists replied by a new wave of crimes—crimes under common law which would have fallen within the jurisdiction of the civil courts if Gildo had not protected the Circumcellions because they supported him in his aim of separating Africa from the Empire.

Traps were laid for Augustine on the roads he had to travel in carrying out his ministry. One day he fell into the hands of the Circumcellions, who were satisfied with beating him severely. Another day an ambush was made, this time with the intention of killing him, but he did not follow his customary route back to Hippo and thus escaped the danger.

The Donatist bishop Petilianus covered Augustine with foul abuse. Augustine replied:

"If I render injury for injury, we would both be guilty. I am not trying to win a victory over another man but to destroy an error. We are not dealing here with the merits of a human being but with the truth of Holy Church. If we must not believe the praises of a friend neither must we believe in the slanders of an enemy. When I am seeking the lost sheep of my Master, is it a cause for astonishment that I am bitten by venomous serpents?"

Stilicho brought grain to Rome from Gaul and Spain and made preparations for the reconquest of the "wheat provinces" of Africa. He had Gildo proclaimed a public enemy by the Roman Senate—a sudden recognition of the long ignored authority of that august assembly. Stilicho then sent to Africa a small army commanded by Mascezel, Gildo's brother and mortal enemy.

In April 398, Mascezel succeeded in routing a large number of Gildo's troops and putting the rest to flight. Gildo tried to escape by sea but was stopped at the waterfront and forthwith executed. A number of African functionaries who had supported him, together with his friend the Donatist bishop Optatus, suffered the same fate.

Count Heraclianus, Stilicho's envoy, took over the reins of government in Africa. Augustine, wishing to convince his opponents, and not to take advantage of their political defeat, now proposed a public debate to Fortunius, a Donatist bishop. This meeting took place at Tuburcicum and was attended by a noisy crowd of spectators who evidently came to see the lion tamer demolished, and who interrupted the debaters with rude remarks. But Augustine showed himself both a tactful diplomat and a sharp polemist, calling on all the resources of his masterly eloquence.

After the debate, each side remained unconvinced by the other, but promised "to examine the question" zealously.

Had a bridge been made? The answer is no, and the bad faith of the Donatists is evident. They considered Augustine's efforts a sign of weakness. If he was so sure he was right, why did he wish to discuss the matter, and why would he try to convince his opponents by persuasive words when the Empire and its armies were on African soil to impose the law against Donatism by force?

Augustine was angry. When Crispinus (whom he had known in Carthage and who had just been elected Donatist bishop of Calama) let it be known that he "would be pleased to meet Augustine," the latter replied: "You are too inclined to misrepresent what is said," and refused any communication except in the form of an exchange of public letters.

From a remote corner of Caesarea in Mauretania, Augustine received a letter from a certain Vincent, a former friend of his, who had joined a Donatist sect known as the Rogatists. Vincent wrote he did not believe that anyone could be *forced* to return to the unity of Christ. In his lengthy reply Augustine quoted the words of the householder in Christ's parable: "Whomsoever you shall find, compel them to come in." He went on to say that he himself had not wished to use any "other arms than prayer and reason" against heresy, since he believed that violent measures of conversion only led the heretics to disguise themselves as Catholics. For a long time he had held to this opinion in spite of pressure from other bishops, but the horrors that had taken place now led him to think otherwise.

"Why should not the earthly kings who serve Christ," he wrote to the Donatists, "not make laws in favor of Christ, since your unjust leaders exposed Caecilian and his brothers to the anger of the temporal authorities of his day?"

He was reluctant to have recourse to the African governor despite the fact that several church councils which met in Carthage had asked the emperor to pass laws against the Donatists. "What!" he exclaimed. "In that case we run the risk of exposing ourselves daily to death at the hands of fanatics."

But was it unreasonable that the Donatists should see turned against them the very weapons they themselves had forged?

Parmenianus, a speaker for the Circumcellions, cried out: "We are martyrs!"

Augustine replied: "You say you are martyrs! If a criminal punished by the State is a martyr, then the prisons are full of martyrs. If you tell us, 'We suffer for our faith,' we could reply, 'Why do you suffer, and what is this faith you speak of?'"

Speaking of the heresy of conferring the sacrament of baptism a second time, he said: "The value of the sacraments is *objective* no matter what the merit of those who administer them." Penance was enough to make a deserter from the faith a Catholic again. Since the Church is composed of the just and of sinners, the value of the sacraments does not depend upon the worthiness of men.

Moreover, how could Christians condone the violence, murders and arson committed by the Circumcellions? Why should they condone the evils which the Donatist Bishop Optatus had perpetrated throughout Africa?

"The law forbids you to rebaptize, but it does not call for

your execution. Now it is the shedding of blood which makes
martyrs and *you* are the ones who shed blood.

"On looking at the list of condemned among your number,
I see only bandits who, armed to the teeth, have gone through
Africa in every direction committing crimes of all kinds—
murder, rape, and other abominable outrages. All this was accomplished under the banner of your religion, and you call
yourselves martyrs!

"You protest against your 'persecution' by the secular power.
Then why did you yourselves persecute the Catholics with
such violence when, with Gildo's support, you were in power
yourselves?"

Having said these things, Augustine did everything to fa-
cilitate the return of the schismatics to the Church. He tried
to protect them in the posts they occupied and to save their
self-respect. He permitted repentant members of the clergy
to return to the Church with the same rank they held before
they rebelled. He asked the faithful to welcome the erring
back among them.

Restitutus, a Catholic priest, was assassinated by the Circumcellions. They gouged out his eyes and cut off the hands
of another priest. The Donatist responsible for these crimes
was captured and condemned to death by the magistrate. Augustine begged the proconsul of Africa to show mercy to this
man, saying: "We do not seek to revenge ourselves on our
enemies. We must not lose sight of the teaching of Him in
whose name we suffer. Forget that you have power over life
and death. Even if I were not a bishop and you did not occupy your exalted post, I would always feel I could turn to
you with the greatest confidence."

He remembered that once he himself had denied God and
the Scriptures, had embraced the diabolical errors of the Manichaeans, the atheistic teachings of Cicero and the philosophical ideas of Plato and Plotinus. Each time he had hoped and
even believed he had touched the garment of Truth. Perhaps
the Donatists also had thought this, and in any case, was it

the role of a civil magistrate to bring them back to the true faith?

When Augustine preached in the basilica, the Donatists flocked to hear him. It was because he spoke as no one else.

"My aim is not to force men to enter this or that communion despite themselves. It is to make known the Truth to all those who seek it."

While Augustine fought the Donatists in Africa, momentous events were taking place elsewhere in the Empire. Stilicho, the regent of the Empire of the West, won Alaric, the mercenary general, to his side, hoping to make allies of the Goths. But Empress Eudoxia (proclaimed Augusta of the Eastern Empire on January 9, 400), despite the fact she was the daughter of a Germanic general, adopted an anti-German policy. Even so, it was necessary to reenlist the barbarians in the army because the Empire could no longer either do without them or defend itself against them. The state of the finances of the government in Milan, later in Ravenna, did not permit it to equip regular troops who demanded too much pay. The army contractors subsidized the emperor, and their fortunes grew to enormous size while the imperial treasury was stripped.

Because of the anti-German policy of the court of Constantinople, the barbarians pressed down upon the West. In the autumn of 401, Alaric and his Visigoths entered Italy and marched on Milan, the seat of the court.

Since the army in Italy had to combat an invasion of Vandals and Alans, Stilicho had to recall troops in haste from Britain and the Rhineland frontier. He defeated the Vandals and forced Alaric, in February 402, to raise the siege of Milan. The Goths continued on their way westward, probably with the intention of invading Gaul. On April 6, 402, the Romans made a surprise attack on the enemy camp and captured the family of Alaric, who immediately concluded an armistice ac-

cording to the terms of which the Goths would evacuate Italy
without delay.

The Emperor Honorius and his court now installed themselves definitively in Ravenna, where they had found refuge
during the siege of Milan. At the end of 403, Honorius arrived
in Rome to celebrate his "victory." The emperor's visit rejoiced the hearts of the Romans, who hoped it would lead to
better treatment for them. As his cortege traveled toward
the Palatine a great crowd assembled to greet him and watched
as he rode by in the triumphal chariot which he shared with
Stilicho. The crowd gaped at the unheard-of splendor of his
crown and the gorgeous jewels he wore. The Roman matrons
looked with tender eye upon this Augustus of nineteen, Theodosius' son.

The sight of the legions, which some years ago had de-
serted the capital, aroused the wild enthusiasm of the people,
who suddenly felt safe and reassured. The legionaries crossed
the Forum, mounted the Via Sacra and conducted the emperor to the palace of Septimus Severus.

As for Alaric, he was waiting behind the Alps for a favorable opportunity to invade Italy again. Toward the end of
405 a horde of barbarians crossed the Alps under the leadership of Radagaisus, a Gothic chief. Stilicho had hastily to
call in as his allies the troops of Uldin the Hun and of the
Goth Sarus. Due to this combination of forces, Radagaisus
was made prisoner on August 23, 406, and his Goths sur-
rendered and were sold as slaves. However, hardly had this
danger been surmounted when another horde of Alans and
Vandals flung themselves against the frontiers of the Rhine.
The federated Franks put up loyal resistance, but in vain; on
December 31, 406, the barbarians crossed the Rhine and over-
ran Gaul.

At this time were sundered the last ties that bound Britain
to the Empire. The Roman troops in Britain were sent to
Gaul and the natives were left to deal as best they could with
the Picts from the north and various German invaders com-

ing by sea. Refugees from the Isle came to the mainland and established themselves on the Armorican peninsula (Brittany).

Alaric's hour had come. When the loyal army, headed by Sarus, was also sent to Gaul, the Visigoth chief passed the Alps and the Po and advanced to the walls of Ravenna. Here he demanded the payment of four thousand pounds of gold for services he had earlier rendered the Empire.

Stilicho's enemies (particularly the pagans) were tireless in their efforts to turn the emperor against him. As Honorius was reviewing troops in Pavia, soldiers attacked the high dignitaries of the court in the emperor's entourage and slew them. When Stilicho, who was in Bologna, heard of this he wanted to march with Sarus against Pavia. However, when he heard Honorius was alive, he abandoned the plan. This so enraged Sarus, who considered Stilicho's failure to act as cowardice, that he turned his Gothic troops against Stilicho's Huns, and great carnage took place. Stilicho sought refuge in Ravenna, but on his arrival he was arrested and decapitated. His son Eucherius also was slain, and Honorius immediately repudiated the empress, who was Stilicho's daughter.

After Stilicho's death, Honorius made ineffective attempts to resist the pressure of the barbarians. Of all the Germans, Sarus remained most faithful to the Empire because his most deadly enemy was Alaric. The latter now marched on Rome, laid siege to the Eternal City, and occupied the port of Ostia.

Augustine was anxious. He wrote to Olympius, who succeeded Stilicho, and the first minister reassured him. At the same time he promised to do all he could to bring about those things that "his friend" Augustine asked for the good of the Church and the Empire.

The Senate finally succeeded in getting Alaric to evacuate Rome by accepting a treaty that imposed an enormous war contribution on the Romans. The pro-German party was again in a leading position at court and Honorius was obliged to replace the law of November 14, 408, favorable to the

Catholic Church, by a decree authorizing the cults of the
Arians and Donatists.

A new first minister, Jovius, seemed disposed to satisfy
Alaric's exorbitant claims; the Visigoth exacted nothing less
than the cession of Dalmatia and Venitia, two of Italy's rich-
est and most fertile provinces.

The Balkan peninsula had been completely laid waste under the occupation of the barbarians, who had no aptitude for
cultivating the lands turned over to them. It was feared the
same thing would occur in the provinces of northern Italy
and the Adriatic. Fortunately the arrival of a massive army of
ten thousand Huns, enrolled in the service of the emperor,
led Alaric to moderate his demands and prevent this coming
about.

Augustine continued his task of building a Christian philosophy. He tirelessly reinforced his bastion with fortifications
of all kinds—historical recollections, allusions to contem-
porary events, references and comparisons to every form of
man's activity, metaphysical speculations, examples in art and
science, and also in nature, well before Francis of Assisi.

Augustine was in the forefront of the combat, and his life
was consecrated to the struggle. He knew that he was useful,
and his work was almost always of immediate service. Each
book he wrote appeared precisely at the right moment and in
answer to a need.

His dialogues were always clever and sparkling. He avoided
abstract discussion, and was at his best when confronted by a
set formula believed to be perfect and in which he uncovered
a flaw that permitted him to demolish the whole structure.
He liked to refute a pamphlet paragraph by paragraph, to
debate, point by point, with another orator before the public.
He moved in directly on his opponents, either to convince or
to refute.

According to him the Christian orator must *understand, ex-
pose and persuade* but never "have as his aim personal suc-

cess or the mere entertainment of his listeners." He should teach what was good, turn other men from evil, convert his opponents, strengthen the weak and enlighten the ignorant. If necessary, he should begin by winning the sympathy of the public, gaining its attention and respect; then he should explain clearly the matter at hand, proving doubtful points and moving his listeners' wills if it were a question of obtaining agreement.

He should know grammar, Latin of course, Greek and, if possible, Hebrew. Augustine likewise attached great importance to history and chronology, to geography and natural history, and to a knowledge of the places and animals, trees and plants mentioned in the Bible.

The orator, he said, should not be ignorant of the mechanical arts. Augustine speaks of learning rhetoric (to train the memory), but insists on dialectics, the science of reasoning, which permits the exegete to deal exactly with the questions that arise from a study in depth of the Bible.

Then he recommends the study of mathematics, arithmetic, geometry, music and mechanics.

This cycle of studies is crowned by philosophy. The Christian should assimilate those ideas of the classical thinkers which are in accordance with the true faith.

Such is the program of "preparatory culture" which Saint Augustine proposed to the Christian intellectual who wishes to be able to draw the greatest possible benefit from the study of the Bible. This program he was to develop at length in his treatise *On Christian Doctrine*.[1]

But in addition to his writings, there were his daily activities. This scholar, who had formerly exchanged ideas only with his companions and disciples, now had to adapt himself to every kind of audience, and in this he was successful. He took into account not only circumstances but the character of his listeners. He weighed everything—words, antitheses, connections, resemblances, touches of humor. In a way, in his writing and his preaching, he acted as a reporter of the combat being waged. At times this is evident from his style in its use of popular expressions or repetitions. He made concessions to his audience in order to hold their interest and used devices that we would call today the element of suspense.

He mixed the Latin of scholars and orators with that of the street and of the professions. The main thing was to find the word to hit the target. He would discuss law with a Roman advocate, or exegesis with a theologian from Alexandria. He argued like a Platonist, told an anecdote like a burgher of Carthage, and castigated the misdeeds of the Circumcellions in the round language of a Hippo dockhand.

St. Augustine's sermons opened up a new era in Christian preaching. There is no doubt he had great powers of persuasion and knew how to speak to men's hearts, but what we would stress here is his admirably direct and intimate style. Whether he was preaching about Jesus on the cross, or denouncing greed and avarice, or explaining and praising the mystery of the Trinity, he was using a new oratorical language.[2]

When he preached a sermon, he would often begin by speaking disparagingly of himself.

"God knows with what trembling I stand before you in His presence. . . . How can we hope to express in passing words the eternal Word of God? And how can a poor instrument like myself be worthy to explain the grandeur of the infinite? The heavens praise Him and the great lights of the firmament and of the stars manifest His glory, so we on earth must praise Him as we can and try to explain and understand Him who in His greatness orders all things."

Before Augustine's day the words of the Fathers of the Church had been sadly influenced by the flowery language of the decadence. Tertullian can be criticized for his tortuous metaphors and Saint Cyprian for his use of verbal ornamentation. Vestiges of these things are still to be found in certain of Augustine's discourses, but what strenuous efforts he made to draw close to his listeners! He strove to combine the ideals of Christian oratory, as he conceived them to be, with their practical application to daily life.[3]

Still following the Socratic method, he asked questions constantly and overcame the objections of hypothetical interlocutors in order to lead them to a reconsideration of the matters they had contested. He observed these interlocutors to discover what it was they knew as certain, and from this point he would lead them to what they did not know or would not believe. It was a step-by-step process.

He mixed and piled up syllogisms, dilemmas, legal arguments and quotations from documents, but he never became bogged down in them. His eye was always fixed on an objective, and although he showed various ways in which it could be attained, he knew exactly where he was leading. Whether he was using the demonstrative method or raillery, he had only one aim—the definitive acceptance of the Catholic philosophy and the confusion of the schismatics.

Faustus of Milevis wrote a book attacking the Christian faith. In the book he wrote in reply, *Against Faustus, the Manichaean,* Augustine said: "Is this the cheery Faustus, the pleasant and charming Faustus, I knew before?" He knew perfectly well it was the same Faustus whose mediocrity had so disappointed him in his early days.

A conscientious objector, Faustus was agitating against war because of his hatred for Rome. In replying to him, Augustine said: "War is an unhappy fact and so is death. War is one way of dying, sadder but perhaps more glorious than the other, and a good man is not frightened at dying."

"I know that the crime of war is contrived by the spirit of Evil," Faustus contended. "But that the spirit of Good takes any part in it is inconceivable."

Augustine's answer was: "If man had submitted to God's law, war would never have been. The world should live in harmony and balance, but if the balance is upset, it should be reestablished. The role Moses played in war does not astonish us, because he was obeying God's commands. Rome's great error has been to refuse for so long to admit conquered peoples under the common law. Why are the rights of the City not given to every citizen of the Empire?"

At every turn the Manichaeans showed their bad faith. Of what use was it to try to reason with them, Augustine said, if "every time we quote the writings of the Apostles our adversaries reply that we have falsified the Scriptures?"

Then he continued: "The authority of the Scriptures has been clear and respected since the time of Christ and the dispersion of the Apostles all over the earth. Consider who you are and how little you are able to understand, I will not say of God, but of your own soul. It is not a question of accepting a vain belief but proven certainties. If you cannot do this, at least admit a Truth that holds an essential place in every human intelligence, namely, that God's nature and substance are absolutely immutable and incorruptible.

"Our origin and that of the world, our nature, our end, the spectacle of the universe—all these mysteries cannot be penetrated by human reason. They are great philosophical problems and resemble steep and lofty mountains over which we try in vain to make our way. No side paths open out to us, and we must drag ourselves upward until the hour arrives when faith gives us wings."

According to Augustine, in reading the Scriptures one must seek in these texts their spiritual meaning. God exists. He has created the Universe with providential design. Without recognizing His existence, how can we explain the existence of the universe and the general order that prevails in it, or the fact that in each living being the organs of the body serve to fulfill a definite function and all these organs together permit that being to survive and to reproduce the species?

How would God be God if He was not infinitely just and infinitely good? Who could limit or diminish the power of God, who could neither sin nor err. The supreme deception, of course, is that Evil exists, and manifests itself under various monstrous forms.

Saint Augustine recognized the existence of Evil, for it was the problem of Evil and its origins that had made him hesitate so long to embrace the Christian faith, and which had led him into the errors of Manichaeism. But, taken in itself, each of the things God has created is good. There is indeed a wondrous grandeur and beauty in the whole; everything is created in a harmony of number, measure and weight.

What, therefore, should one think of the evils that befall creatures? Are Lucifer and his devils responsible for such things as death, sorrow and suffering?

The reply is simple: these evils are the punishment for crimes committed by sinful men. If Lucifer was cast into hell, it was because he revolted against God.[4]

Now appears for the first time a clear exposition of Augustine's teaching regarding grace:

"God operates in us to will and act, as Saint Paul says. He grants us His grace purely of His own accord; otherwise it would not be grace, a gift, but something due us. God gives each man faith in the measure He pleases and if He wishes him to be among the saved, he will be saved."

Why does God favor one man and not another? Here again Augustine bases himself on Saint Paul's authority when he said: "God never does anything that is not just. Adam sinned, and since all mankind was present in the first man, all shared in Adam's sin. God owes no one anything, and He cannot be accused of injustice. But because He is kind and merciful, He chooses among men those certain ones who will be saved.

"Why does He choose this man rather than that man? We do not know, because God's ways are impenetrable to human eyes. But the elect cannot glory in their merits nor can those who are lost complain; in the case of the latter, God renders for sin only what is its due."

In the year 400, Augustine began the writing of his Confessions in order to reply in all openness to the attacks being made on him from many sides. The Donatists and the

Manichaeans especially reproached him with his past, his turbulent life, the different beliefs he had held before he became a Catholic.

Augustine's reply is one of the most beautiful books of human thought. It is the story of a soul groping in search for self and in the end finding reality in God.

In the latter part of the book, he is concerned with the problem of wisdom. God, he says, cannot be known by carnal knowledge, which acts only in relation to those things situated in time and space. Now God is outside time, which is a physical act, a distension of the mind. The only reality is the Eternal, which we may picture to ourselves as an eternal Present. God exists in Eternity.

"In the beginning, O God, You made heaven and earth, in Your Word, in Your Power, in Your Wisdom, in Your Truth, speaking in a wondrous way and working in a wondrous way. . . . What is that which shines through me and strikes my heart without injuring it? . . . I both shudder and glow with passion: I shudder, inasmuch as I am unlike it; I glow with passion inasmuch as I am like it.

"It is Wisdom, Wisdom itself which shines through me, cutting through my dark clouds which again cover me over, as I fall down because of that darkness and under the load of my punishments."

This epic work, recounting the inner drama of a soul in the process of its conversion to Christianity, is unique in the literature of all time. The noted French author Daniel-Rops says: "If Augustine speaks of himself or of his failings and his misery it is in order to show by a concrete example the omnipotence of God and of grace. A hundred times the writer interrupts his recital to give voice to the cry of love that mounts to his lips. His book is as much a prayer as it is a confession. The significance of the title *Confessions* extends far beyond that attached to the word confidences, and is to be accepted in its highest meaning in the language of Christianity; it should be understood in the sense that we say a believer *confesses* his faith.

"Several hundred years before Augustine, Heraclitus, the philosopher of the obscure, inscribed among the 333 axioms he wrote down: 'I seek my *I*.' Socrates admitted he was unable to know himself and Aristotle proclaimed that 'the perfect man never speaks of himself.' But since Jesus had said, 'the Kingdom of God is within you,' since Christianity had assigned a unique importance to the individual soul, made in the image and likeness of God, the perspective had changed. One of Augustine's deepest intuitions was to see this. His central idea, very often repeated in the course of his book, was that the interior man is engraved with the image of God. He bears this image in three constituent parts of his being —in his mind, in his conscience, and in his heart, the essence of which Augustine describes as understanding and will.

"Two consequences follow from this profound intuition. The first is that if man enters the deepest part of his being, He will find God. 'O God, let me know myself so that I may know You!'"

In conclusion, Augustine says that man *exists*. He cannot doubt that he *is* and *wills* to be. These certainties are a symbol of the Trinity—absolute Being, who is the Father; absolute Wisdom, who is the Son; and absolute Will for good, who is the Holy Spirit.

"Who among us understands the almighty Trinity? Yet who among us does not speak of it, if it indeed be the Trinity he speaks of? Rare is the soul that knows whereof it speaks, whatsoever it says concerning the Trinity. They contend and they quarrel, but without peace no man sees that vision. I would that men would reflect upon these three things within themselves. Far different are these three from that Trinity, but I indicate where it is men may consider them, weigh them, and perceive how far different they are.

"I speak of these three: to be, to know, and to will. For I am, I know, and I will: I am a knowing and a willing being, and I know that I am and that I will, and I will to be and to know. Therefore, in these three, let him who can do so perceive how inseparable a life there is, one life and one mind and one essence, and finally how inseparable a distinction there is, and yet there is a distinction. Surely a man stands face to face with himself. Let him take heed of himself, and look there, and tell me. But when he has discovered any of these and is ready to speak, let him not think that he has found that immutable Being which is above all these, which is immutably, and knows immutably, and will immutably. . . .

"Who could conceive such things with any ease? Who could state them in any manner? Who could rashly pronounce thereon in any way?"

Augustine found his nourishment in the Scriptures, and in the *Confessions* he exclaims: "O Lord, my God . . . from all temerity and all lying circumcise my lips, both my interior and my exterior lips. May Your Scriptures be my chaste delight! May I never fall into error in my reading of them, may I never deceive others by my use of them. . . .

"Not for nothing have You willed that these deep secrets be written on so many pages. Nor are those forests to lack their harts, who will retire therein and regain their strength, walk about and feed, lie down and ruminate. Lord, perfect me and open those pages to me."

In 404, Felix the Manichaean accepted Augustine's invitation to a debate in the basilica of Hippo before an assemblage of the people. The first meeting took place on December 7, 404, and the second on the twelfth of the same month.

When the member of the Manichaean elect and the Catholic bishop came face to face, Augustine led with a fiery attack. He pressed his opponent hard, scarcely allowing him time to draw breath, and the spectators' attention was riveted to this display of dialectical skill. In the end Felix gave in— and was converted.

In 405, Augustine wrote *On the Nature of Good,* again in answer to the Manichaeans. He kept up an unbroken correspondence with illustrious members of the clergy as with the most humble members of the faithful. To a young girl, Proba, he explained the Lord's Prayer in these words:

"When we say, 'Thy Kingdom come,' we are expressing our desire that this Kingdom may arrive *for us* and that we may be worthy to have a place in it. When we say, 'Thy will be done,' we are asking Him for the grace to be obedient to Him. When we say, 'Give us this day our daily bread,' this means the Sacrament which the faithful receive and which is necessary in this life if we are to win eternal happiness. When we say, 'Forgive us our trespasses,' we recall to our minds what it is we have to do in order to obtain that forgiveness. In saying, 'Lead us not into temptation,' we are warning ourselves that we must implore the Lord's help so that our weakness may not cause us to fall into sin. And when we say, 'Deliver us from evil,' it is to remind us we are not yet in that good estate where we have nothing to fear."

He had a long discussion with Saint Jerome about a passage in Saint Paul's Epistle to the Galatians. This correspondence between Africa and Palestine was not entirely serene. Augustine wrote the illustrious philologist concerning certain objections he had to the latter's new translation of the Bible. Jerome was upset and even irritated. Their correspondence lasted for years because each time either of them wrote the other, he had to find some traveler to take the letter. On both sides these letters were models of the epistolary style of the time, ceremonious, lyrical in expression and "beflowered with allusions to Vergil" and other rhetorical ornaments.

The same polite ceremoniousness prevailed in the letters to Simplicianus, who succeeded Ambrose in Milan in 397, and who was the censor to whom Augustine submitted his books. He also corresponded with high members of the

Catholic aristocracy and in these letters he used an almost worldly style.

He consulted with his friend Paulinus of Nola on serious exegetical and theological questions, and exchanged ideas with Romanianus who had "a great faculty for landing on his feet" despite certain difficulties he had. He replied to letters from Licentius, from Alypius (who, on a journey to the Holy Land, met Jerome and brought him Augustine's greetings and a letter) and even to pagan intellectuals such as Maximus of Madaura. Certain high dignitaries had remained pagans in spite of the laws, and there were still important groups of them in certain professions. Paganism was particularly rife in the theatrical world as well as among teachers of grammar and rhetoric.

Augustine never invoked the law against them, even saving the lives of pagans who had been pointed out to the executioners. He was indignant at the rapacity of certain of the "faithful" who wished to appropriate the property of idolaters.

"What we are trying to do," he said, "is to break the idols in pagan hearts. Those of them who become Christians ask us themselves to break the statues in their gardens."

With the pagan Maximus he exchanged letters on spiritual matters, sprinkled with quotations from Vergil's poems. To Dioscorus he mapped out a detailed study of pagan morality. "What more salutary exchange could there be," he asked, "than for those who know one another and are animated by goodwill to seek together the means of acquiring virtue?"

A great lord, Volusianus, expressed to Augustine his doubts concerning the Incarnation. How could one believe that the Master of the world had dwelled in a virgin's womb? Was it necessary for God to reach manhood by passing slowly through the various stages of life? Such a Man-God would need sleep and food, and what sign would reveal Him to the world?

Augustine had answered just such objections in his *Confessions* when he wrote: "The mediator between God and

man must have something like to God and something like
to men, lest being in both things like to men, he should be
far from God, or being in both ways like to God, he should
be far from men, and so not be a mediator. . . . The true
mediator, whom in Your secret mercy You have shown to be
humble, whom You have sent to them, that by His example
they also might learn humility, that messenger of God and
man, the man Christ Jesus appeared between mortal sinners
and the immortal Just One, mortal with men, just with God."

Now he answered Volusianus' questions with tireless attention and zeal. He was replying to all pagans when he wrote:

"The language of the Scriptures contains so great a depth
of wisdom that the most powerful, able and attentive minds
experience every day the truth of what is said of our Holy
Books: 'When a man believes he has finished, he is only at
the beginning.'"

After a long explanation of God's omnipresence, and the
eternal existence of the Word, Augustine made this point:

"God's greatness is not a greatness of size but of virtue
and power. It was this power which drew forth the body of a
child from Mary's womb. If the Man-God was subject to all
our infirmities it was to prove He was really man. God raised
man up to Himself without going out of Himself and without
ceasing to be God." Then Augustine added that those who
asked the reason for this mystery should first try to explain
their own nature.

On another day, he rose up against the practice of magic.
He thundered out denunciations of the theater which had so
delighted his youth. (Plato had considered "women and
poets" as great dangers for the Republic, and Cicero had opposed the excessive liberty allowed to the Greek playwrights.)
In a sermon preached at Carthage, Augustine said:

"What harm is wrought by a debased curiosity, by the idle
concupiscence of the eyes, by your eagerness for the inanities
offered in the theaters! . . . Is it possible that a debased ex-
hibition can please a good man?"

He had become by degrees the greatest personage of the

Church; only Saint Jerome equaled him in prestige. From
Hippo he guarded the life of Christianity and was the interpreter of Pauline thought. In the world of religion he had
assumed the authority of the ancient Hebrew prophets. He
was consulted on every side and appeared to his contempo-
raries as "a pilgrim from heaven who was questioned by everyone concerning the secret marvels of that unknown country."

He thus became the center of a tremendous movement of
ideas, receiving correspondence from all corners of the Christian world and replying to it with patience and care. He
grasped every occasion to make his opinions known. Confronted with a problem, his first act was to open the Holy
Books—the two Testaments, the Acts of the Apostles, and the
Epistles—seeking to find in them a solution of that problem.

This change of perspective was complete and took place
as a new civilization was dawning. From Augustine would be
born the Christian Middle Ages when all intellectual matters
were placed in dependence on faith. His powerful synthesis
of the thought of the first Doctors of the Church with the
ancient philosophy of Plato and Plotinus laid the foundations
for modern Christianity. He was indeed the "Doctor of the
new era.'"

And now occurred the event that many felt was a mortal
blow to Roman civilization and culture. Alaric marched on
Rome a second time, and forced the Senate to elect a new
emperor in November 409. The emperor was Attalus, a pagan
and Symmachus' friend. On assuming the purple, he became
an Arian and was baptized by the bishop of the Goths.

Because of the necessity of supplying the metropolis with
wheat, Alaric and Attalus were early faced with the task of
bringing under subjection the provinces of Africa where Count
Heraclianus, the governor, remained loyal to Honorius. Attalus declined Alaric's offer to undertake the conquest of
Africa because he feared that once the Goths had crossed
the sea to this rich country, they would not leave it.

To Heraclianus was sent a "successor" guarded by a handful of Roman soldiers, who embarked for Algiers. At the same time Attalus marched on Ravenna with his Goths. Honorius proposed to recognize him as an emperor of second rank, but Attalus believed he had the whip hand and demanded Honorius' abdication as emperor. The Gothic army had encamped before the wall of Ravenna and Honorius was at the point of flight when an army of four thousand men, sent by Antemius, the regent of the East, arrived by sea to Honorius' relief. Attalus was completely defeated and fled from the scene.

The attempt to take over Africa was thwarted by Count Heraclianus, whose would-be successor was slain with his troops on the beach at Algiers. On his return to Rome from Ravenna, Attalus still refused to send the Gothic troops to Africa. This led to the dissolution of the alliance between the Goths and Attalus with his Romans.

Alaric made a third march on Rome and this time the city fell into his hands, on August 24, 410. For three days the Goths sacked the city, violating, burning and slaying. Incomparable treasures were lost, priceless works of art destroyed; assassinations, mass carnage, torture and mutilations followed in turn. When Alaric decided it was time to reassemble his soldiers, he gave the signal to depart. It was not his intention to annex the Empire; he was but a rebel mercenary who for a time had turned over the pillage of a great city to his henchmen. Nevertheless, to many men the capture and sack of Rome was a calamity, the symbol of the end of its greatness.

The news soon crossed the Mediterranean, and Augustine wrote Italica, a pious woman of Rome, asking the truth of "the sad rumors spread throughout Africa," so that he might "place himself in community of spirit with the faithful of Rome in their sufferings and trials."

Actually the news of Alaric's capture of Rome had resounded as a clap of thunder in Roman Africa. On all sides one heard: "The barbarians are coming! The barbarians are here!" Fugitives arriving from Rome, no one knew how, told of irreparable disasters, for, in the eyes of Hannibal's descendants, Rome had immense prestige and was the center of the world.

When Augustine heard the terrible news was true, he was horrified and distraught. Roman culture and glory were dear to his heart, and he foresaw that the collapse of the Empire would result in violent upheaval and lead the old world back into barbarism.

Again he wrote Italica. "Your letter tells me nothing of what transpired in Rome. Perhaps you have not told us for fear of saddening us? It would, nevertheless, be useful for us to know, because it is not right for us to enjoy ourselves when others are suffering, and not to join our tears with yours."

The duties of charity had never seemed more imperious to him. The exiles must be made welcome, clothed and fed, work found for them, and their dignity as men restored. The most exemplary Christian charity must be shown toward these victims of barbarism.

"Do not forget," Augustine said to his people, "that in every poor man we must see Christ. How can we see this man dying of cold, in exile? As for ourselves, we must not lose hope. Even were the world to disappear, the Christian should fear nothing.

"I hear you say, 'We are cursed, the end of the world has come!' Heaven and earth will pass away, but God's Word will not pass away. Your real life cannot be taken from you by the barbarians; man's true lot is not to weep but to build for tomorrow."

At Hippo, Augustine wrote at the top of a blank page the title of a new book he would write: *City of God*.

The wind of history was rising and giving birth to a tempest which was not to be delayed for long.

Chapter Nine

THE CITY OF GOD
AND THE BARBARIANS
410-426

Augustine was now fifty-six, more and more shrunken and dried in appearance. His voice was often hoarse, his face furrowed with deep wrinkles. He was prematurely aged by sleepless nights and exhausting work and by his poor health, which he had never spared.

His skin was almost black, his hair and long beard already white. His head was tonsured and he wore a long black robe with a cowl. When the members of the faithful presented him with better clothing he sold it and gave the money to the poor. He did not want to differ in his dress from the other priests of his diocese and accepted only such gifts as might serve the community.

"It is no doubt permissible," he said, "for a bishop with a private fortune to wear costly clothing, but would you want people to say that I found in the Church the means to dress myself better than I could have done in my father's house? A rich dress is no more appropriate when I carry out my obligation to preach than the worn-out body and white hair you see before you."

His residence in Hippo was a monastery in which the clergy lived on revenues held in common and where all submitted to the same rule. A priest of the community, one

Januarius, revealed on his deathbed that he had put aside a certain sum of money, intending to bequeath his little hoard to the diocese of Hippo. Augustine refused the legacy and preached a sermon in which he said that having given all clergy the right to choose their mode of existence, he would release those who found community life unsuited to them, but he would strike from the list of his clergy anyone who possessed private property.

Before entering the community a certain deacon had purchased several slaves. "This deacon," Augustine decided, "must free those slaves today in your presence before being allowed to join you."

In the Christian communities of that period the relationship between priests and faithful was close, almost family-like. The people kept a watchful eye on each member of the clergy and even mixed constantly in ecclesiastical matters. Augustine fell in with such customs, considering that since the Christians had shown their confidence in him he should give them an accounting of his stewardship as one who had been elected to the office he held.

His meals and those of his companions consisted of vegetables; meat was not served unless there were guests. They took wine, but in moderation. The dishes and utensils used at table were of earthenware or marble, but they ate with silver spoons that Augustine had presented to the community.

When a priest took God's name in vain, he was deprived of wine at meals, lest a small oath should lead to more serious perjury. If the bishop had some criticism to make to one of his brothers, he spoke to him in private. He said repeatedly that the sinner who sincerely repents must be forgiven not seven times but seventy-seven.

Old Jerome had said: "You should allow women to pass the threshold of your humble dwelling but seldom." Augustine still held in terror the temptations of the flesh, and no woman lived in his house, not even his sister who, after being widowed, had consecrated herself to God and was in charge of a religious community. Augustine never spoke to a woman except in the presence of a third person. He left the door of his room open all day, as he had seen Ambrose do in Milan, so that anyone might enter who needed his help.

Possidius, his biographer, tells us that the bishop of Hippo wrote and dictated so many books and letters it would be difficult for even the most studious reader to cover them all in a single lifetime. This was because Augustine knew better than other men how to arrange his time, and left no part of his schedule unfilled.

He wished to be relieved of the details of diocesan administration, but this was impossible. It was true he had put the material management of the house into the hands of a cleric who submitted to him an account of receipts and expenses at the end of each month, but everything else he had to take care of himself.

When the Church had no funds, he would simply say to the faithful: "I have nothing more to give to the poor." To prevent the poor from dying of hunger, to ransom the captive, and to purchase land where Christians might be buried, were the three reasons that on several occasions he ordered sacred vessels to be broken and melted down.

"It is better to save souls for the Lord than to save gold," he said. "The most precious vessels are those which deliver souls from death. The Lord's real treasure lies in the operation of His own precious blood."

Burdened with all these temporal obligations, he envied the lot of the monks of the desert, and often congratulated the cenobites who visited his monastery on the way of life they had chosen. He had a taste for manual labor and would have liked to divide his life between physical activity and study. He could not understand how certain monks could remain idle.

"I wonder how those monks who do no work are able to fill up their time!" he exclaimed. "Is it with prayer, chanting, reading the Word of God? It may be so; but if they do not

sometimes interrupt these occupations, whence comes their
food? Even the birds feed themselves unless they are caged."

All this while, refugees continued to pour in from Italy,
and the great upheaval caused by the invasion of the barbarians had hardened many hearts—a return to brute instincts
had accompanied the catastrophe.

"The invasion does not release us from the laws of justice!"
cried the bishop of Hippo. "With all its horror, it is still
within the designs of Providence. What do we know of what
God intends in His omnipotence, in His mercy? There are
tears which are prayers, and sufferings which play a part in
redemption."

Augustine nevertheless saw a terrible moral danger in
torpid despair and resignation. "What," he cried, "you learn
that people in Eastern lands are weeping over your misfortunes, and you run to the theaters! As each wave of bad news
reaches you, the fever rises and you make every attempt to
forget at no matter what cost."

What Augustine had hoped to see instead was an upsurge
of faith in men's souls. But the morale of those who surrounded him was bad, and on every side he heard cursing
and weeping. Pagans and Christians blamed each other for
the disaster and, as always, great misfortune had the effect of
bringing buried enmities to the surface.

One of his friends believed the end of the world was at
hand. He wrote asking Augustine for his opinion, and the
bishop was troubled. Nothing was more calculated than this
despairing supposition to demoralize men's souls and make
them forget their duties to suffering Rome and to perscuted
Christianity at the very moment when all their energies were
needed. If people were convinced that before the barbarians
came, Christ would appear and the world would end, they
would make no effort to help others. "Rome is not lost if the
Romans are not lost," Augustine said. "But they are certainly
lost if they continue in their blasphemies."

Rome was not a pile of stones and rubble. She lived on in

the souls of her children, and souls do not die. The fatherland had a soul, and if its citizens would look into their consciences and rediscover the virile virtures of their race, Rome would be saved. The living soul of a people was a treasure that no pillager could steal.

A Christian State is not a nation ruled by Christ through His religious representatives, but a nation ruled by Him from within the inner consciences of its leaders, magistrates and citizens. Of Christian rulers Augustine said in *City of God*:

"We call those Christian emperors happy who govern with justice, who are not puffed up by the tongues of flatterers or the services of sycophants, but remember that they are men. . . . We call them happy when they are slow to punish, quick to forgive; when they punish, not out of private revenge, but only when forced by the order and security of the republic."

Authority was difficult to maintain, Augustine said. But he who rules must first command himself. He must guard against the terrifying dangers that beset him who leads, especially pride in thinking he is first, and against a passion to dominate. "For a man to tell himself that God alone is great and he is but a man, even when he commands millions of other men—nothing is more difficult and nothing is more necessary." For such a leader to believe himself a being superior to those he governs is to lower himself in their eyes, for pride is followed by all other forms of degradation.

"Do you not know that it takes only a little yeast to sour the dough? The passion to dominate is as corrupting as pride. It consists in wielding authority as a personal possession which one can either use or abuse as he wishes. The most evident of these abuses is to curtail the liberty of others. Men have grouped themselves into cities and kingdoms in order to be stronger, more at peace, and to enjoy happiness. Their leader must try to do all he can to supply these things which are necessary to men and, in a word, to act as their Providence."

Since the Roman world was in danger, Augustine showed himself strongly patriotic and referred to Plato, who said:

"It is the fatherland which has given us birth, nourished and reared us. It is for us more precious than our father, our mother or our ancestors. We must suffer without protest and die without complaint, if the fatherland wishes us to suffer and to die."

When Christianity had spread over the world, Rome had accepted the practice of the religion of Christ and had borne at the same time the responsibilities of the State. No longer was the Kingdom of God in opposition to the earthly kingdom. Saint Ambrose had codified Christian morals and included in its proper place the duties of a citizen.

Augustine argued in principle that a Christian is better equipped than others to serve his country. "It was at Christ's order that Peter carried a sword, and if he returned it to its scabbard at the request of his Master, it was because that Master did not wish to be defended."

Soldiers were the guardians of order, the defenders of justice. The peace preached by Christ supposed soldiers to defend it. David, the holy prophet, had been a soldier.

With these theses, Augustine began the writing of his greatest work. He was to take ten years to complete the *City of God.*

The bodies of Peter and Paul were in Rome, where innumerable other martyrs were buried, and now Rome was devastated. For Augustine this was something more than a cause for lamentations. His reaction had, as was almost always true in his case, a "polemical" cause. He seized upon this dramatic and shattering event to lay down the bases of a philosophy of history.

The pagans had arisen to proclaim that if Rome had been demolished and pillaged, it was the fault of Christianity. In the days of the gods, Rome had flourished because the emperors were descendants of those gods. Now the gods had abandoned Rome and it would perish.

What was Augustine's reply? First, that the devastation

and massacres perpetrated by the Goths were afflictions sent down on those Christians who were too greatly attached to earthly goods. Next, he said that numerous moral and physical calamities had befallen Rome in times when the gods were freely worshiped. It was divine Providence and not the dangerous materialism of the Epicureans nor the fatalism of the Stoics which had made the Roman Empire great.

Augustine began a violent criticism of the pagan religion, refuting with fervor the natural theology built up by the pagan philosophers: before Socrates there was a total lack of comprehension of God's immateriality; in Plato's case there was ignorance of the fact of the Redemption; in the case of the Neoplatonists, the impossibility of reconciling their demonology with divine Omnipotence.

Paganism was a religion of theatrical display. In the hands of the poets, its mythology was blown up and combined, as the occasion required, with vague mysticism and complicated symbolism. In passing, Augustine berated the pagan "rites," especially their sacrifices, which were real scenes of butchery as herds of oxen were killed on the temple pavements, their throats slit in such numbers it was impossible to count the heads. He recalled the millions of white birds, doves or gulls, massacred not so long before by order of the Emperor Julian. Under Caligula, within three months more than a hundred and sixty thousand animals were immolated in Rome in sacrifices that took place before the populace, which demanded them loudly and participated in these mad scenes. These hecatombs were carried out on the temple courts, in forums, at the feet of statues splashed with blood.

Still more abominable were the practices of divination—the laying bare of the entrails of animals and reading a prophetic meaning into them. Augustine denounced these "sacrifices of offal" and contrasted with them "the pure oblation of the Eucharistic bread and wine."

He thundered against the paganism which allowed the

morals of its worshipers to sink so low and which laid down no precepts for them.

"The worshipers and admirers of these gods delight in imitating their scandalous iniquities, and are no wise concerned that the republic be less depraved and licentious. Only let it remain undefeated, they say, only let it flourish and abound in resources; let it be glorious by its victories, or better still, secure in peace; and what matters it to us?

"This is our concern, that every man be able to increase his wealth so as to supply his daily prodigalities, and so that the powerful may subject the weak for their purposes. Let the poor court the rich for a living, that under their protection they may enjoy a sluggish tranquillity; and let the rich abuse the poor as their dependents, to minister to their pride. Let the people applaud not those who protect their interests, but those who provide them with pleasure. Let no severe duty be commanded, no impurity forbidden. . . . Let the provinces stand loyal to the governors, not as moral guides but as lords of their people and purveyors of their pleasures; not with a hearty reverence, but a crooked and servile fear.

"Let the laws take cognizance rather of the injury done to another man's property, than that done one's own person. In his own affairs let everyone with impunity do what he will. . . . Let there be a plentiful supply of public prostitutes for everyone who wishes to use them, but especially for those who are too poor to keep one for their private use. . . .

"Let there be provided the most sumptuous banquets where everyone who pleases may, by day or night, play, drink, vomit, dissipate. Let there be heard everywhere the rustling of dancers, the loud, immodest laugh of the theater; let a succession of the most cruel and voluptuous pleasures maintain a perpetual excitement. If such excitement is distasteful to any, let him be branded as a public enemy. . . . Let these be reckoned as true gods, who procure for the people this condition of things, and preserve it when once possessed. . . .

"No, all this is not worthy to survive! It is not the abandonment of these practices which has caused the decadence of the Empire. If you ask that the temples of these gods be opened anew, it is only because they are indulgent to your vices. In your hearts you mock them and the Empire as well. There is the true cause of decadence. . . .

"But it is now day; awake as you awoke in the persons of those men in whose sterling virtues and sufferings for the faith we glory. They battled on all sides against hostile powers and, conquering by their fearless death, 'have purchased the country for us with their blood.' To this country we pleadingly invite you. Join its citizens, for it offers more than mere sanctuary, it offers the true remission of your sins."

Augustine passed in burlesque review the cortege of gods assigned to each stage of life and those for all stages: the insignificant divinities who caused wheat to grow, those who watched over children, who assisted women in labor, who guarded doors, thresholds, hinges, the god who watched the consummation of wedlock. "For pity sake," Augustine exclaims, "why did they not leave the husband something to do!"

In the next part of the *City of God* he elaborates a theology of history. His thesis may be described as the struggle between two rival cities which have existed and will exist in opposition to each other throughout all time, from the fall of Lucifer and Adam's sin to the end of the world. The City of God is the eternal kingdom of the saved; the Earthly City is the city of the devil.

He shows how time had its origin with the Creation of the world since eternity does not change at all and "there could have been no time had not a creature been made whose movement would effect some change." He then comes to a consideration of the origins and characteristics of the two cities.

Cain and Abel were the fathers of the two cities of heaven and of earth. Cain, the founder of the worldly city, murdered his brother.

As a former Manichaean, Augustine was quite at home in

this realm of ideas: the carnal city is centered around love of self; the spiritual city around the love of God. Each has its own way of life, and each has developed down through the generations, as the Bible tells.

Moses is a mystical prefiguration of the City of God during its passage through earth. After Noah and the dispersion of peoples, the Earthly City developed in the great Eastern kingdoms, in Greece, then in ancient Rome. Providence made use of Rome in order to assemble divers nations under the same laws, and thus prepared for the coming of Jesus Christ.

In the last part of his work, Augustine studies the question of happiness and of the necessity of its foundation on the divine. Worldly life is but disorder, passion and violence. All depends on God's judgment, and in its light, vice will be revealed for what it is even if it has been disguised under the aspect of virtue. At the Last Judgment the two cities will be separated. The city of the world will enter an eternity of physical and moral suffering; the elect of the City of God will know eternal happiness.

In the *City of God*, Augustine, the exegete, metaphysician and psychologist, expands, sometimes in rather diffuse fashion, all the theses of his previous books. His anti-Manichaeism, anti-Donatism, anti-Pelagianism (of which we shall speak later) impede at times the flow of this remarkable piece of writing—but what does this matter, in view of the perspective this book was to open to future historians!

Due to him, the Bible would take its place in universal history and would serve as its thread. The lessons of the Scripture would give meaning to the march of history itself, and the Christian would at last be shown the golden string that leads from the Creation of the world to the Day of Judgment.[1]

In the course of this outline of a philosophy of history, Augustine undoubtedly included a concept of the evolution of mankind: "Man alone," he says, "makes the line of division between the children of God and the children of the devil.

"In my view, in the first man created in the beginning, there was established, not as yet indeed in actual appearance but in the foreknowledge of God, the origin of these two cities or societies, so far as concerns the human race. From this first man were to come all men, some to be associated with the bad angels in their punishment and others to be fellow citizens with the good angels in their rewards. . . .

"A thin stream of pure water flows across the history of man. God inspires in certain men faith, love of His Person, and the desire to imitate His sublime qualities; these He purifies by His grace and saves. All those who participate in this Good, form between themselves and with Him they love a holy and blessed society, the City of God. Beside them is an immense wave of others who have been called but have not been chosen.

"Final happiness will be for the good. Let us therefore pray God to grant us the necessary grace to enter into the stream of the elect on their way to the heavenly City. Let us beg that faith, that hope, and that charity which are the mark and consolation of the Christian. No one will be lost who has faith and hope, no one can think he is abandoned who has faith in Jesus, since He lives within his heart. We need nothing more than faith, hope, and charity to be enlightened as to the meaning of human history. Man acts; God guides."

Revival of paganism, massacre of Christians, troubles in Calama where houses belonging to the Church were burned, battles in the streets of Carthage between Christians and pagans, oracles predicting that, after a reign of three hundred and sixty-five years, Christianity would be finally vanquished —such is the first summation of this first quarter of the fifth century.

Vandals, Alans and Suevi crossed the Pyrenees, and, passing into Spain, seized the western part of the peninsula and forced the Emperor Honorius to come to terms with them. In the meanwhile Jovinus, a nobleman of Gaul, was pro-

claimed emperor in Germany and, supported by the Burgundians and Alans, was quickly recognized by the Franks
in Gaul and Brittany. In 412 the Visigoths penetrated into
Gaul under the leadership of Ataulf, Alaric's brother-in-law.
Sarus, the Goth, was again on bad terms with the court at
Ravenna and went to Gaul to join Jovinus, but was killed by
the Visigoths.

By imperial edict the Catholic and Donatist bishops met
at Carthage under the presidency of the tribune Marcellinus,
the emperor thus making a last effort to reestablish the unity
of the Church in Africa. On May 18, 411, the Donatist prelates made their entrance into Carthage in pompous array.
There were two hundred and seventy-eight of them, whereas
the Catholic bishops were two hundred and eighty-six in number.

Augustine preached the opening sermon. "Pray for the
bishops," he said. "The bishops are debating for your sake.
And give alms to the poor. Alms are the wings on which
prayer ascends to God."

Marcellinus decided that a commission limited to eighteen
bishops of each party should meet in the hall of the Baths of
Gargilius in the center of the city. Here he read to them
Honorius' edict, signed at Ravenna. Immediately the Donatists began to put up opposition and make delays, wrangling
over signatures and protocol, showing themselves in general
as masters of the art of obstruction.

Every day throughout the whole conference Augustine had
to defend himself against slanderous charges circulated in
pamphlets throughout the city, and against the most frightful
calumnies spread verbally. At first he countered all this with
the aloofness of a man who had nothing to fear, but the
Donatists wanted to annihilate him at no matter what cost.
Basically they knew what they were doing, for if they succeeded in striking down the Catholic leader they would have
a chance to triumph. Therefore their target was Augustine,

and certain of his opponents were adept at flattering the people and raking up prejudices and gossip hurtful to him.

The calumniators were not discouraged by public opinion, which enjoyed the spectacle of a great man subjected to such an assault. He was accused, for instance, of being a meddler and mixing in everybody's business. This only made people smile, but more venom was raised by the sneering reminder that Augustine had earlier been a Manichaean (who knew, perhaps, but that he was still one in disguise?). It was also whispered that he was a lover of women. Had he not had a concubine and a natural child?

Faced with this avalanche of slander, Augustine was obliged to defend himself vigorously. He gave facts and dates. Certain people remained skeptical, even certain of those among his friends and acquaintances. "Calumniate and you will exasperate," St. Basil was to say. And so it was. Augustine found words to convince men of good faith and to silence the others. He did not give up an inch of the ground he gained; a born polemist, he was perfectly at ease in this battle. He knew it was the Church that was being attacked through him. In replying, he made attacks himself, pulverizing the Donatist leaders of whose weaknesses, foolishness, and surrender of principle he was well aware. It was not he who had sought such grounds of discussion or had chosen polemics of this kind, but he showed he feared no one when he took up his pen to make written replies to charges or when he faced the tribune in person.

Despite all this, the question of doctrine was reached. On June 8 came Augustine's turn to speak. The main question, he said, was to know which of the two parties was the true Catholic Church. To answer, it was necessary to go back to the old quarrel over Caecilian. Nevertheless, Caecilian's innocence had been adjudged by the Councils of Rome and Arles and confirmed by Emperor Constantine the Great.

Since the opening of the conference the bishop of Hippo had carried on his shoulders alone the weight of the battle on every front. That day he dominated all and imposed his solution.

"The eyes of the Christian world," he said, "are fixed on this assemblage in Carthage. The people (and also the Donatists, it would seem) have forgotten the origin of the schism. We have seen the contemptible chicanery of individuals substituted for the great issues of Christian solidarity. When the barbarians are in Rome, when all mankind is eager to learn of the things of God, we are here, engaged in miserable litigation."

In 311 the Carthaginian bishops had condemned Caecilian without a hearing. In 411, one hundred years later, it was the Donatists who were condemned at Carthage at Augustine's behest.

Marcellinus, the tribune who presided at the conference, expressed his hope that so old a wound might be healed. He proclaimed Caecilian's innocence, forbade religious assemblages of the Donatists, ordered their churches to be turned over to the Catholics, "the justice of whose cause is supported by many proofs." Each Donatist bishop could return to his home without fear and then request his reintegration into the Church. All those who had troops of Circumcellions in their dioceses should see to it that they were disarmed at once.

Augustine drew up with his own hand the minutes of the conference. A delay was granted the Donatists to return to the bosom of the Church, a delay after which they would be subject to legal sanctions.

The Donatists appealed to the emperor against this decision, but in reply Honorius promulgated (January 4, 412) a law ordering that all members of the schismatic sect should be subject to heavy fines, that Donatist slaves and colonists should be brought back into the Church, and finally that the Donatist clergy should be deported.

However, it appears that just at this time Count Heraclianus, the governor of Africa (the man who had directed the arrest and execution of Stilicho), laid claim to the imperial purple. Counting on the support of Donatists and Circumcellions, he began to suspend the wheat shipments, as Gildo had done in his day. Moreover, in June 413 he started out with a small flotilla to Italy with the intention of seizing Rome and landed his forces at the mouth of the Tiber. His army was annihilated on the Flaminian Way, and he alone escaped. Returning to Africa, he fell into the hands of Marinus, a general dispatched in his pursuit, and was beheaded at Carthage in the summer of 413.

In his indignation Honorius followed with the most terrible of repressive measures against the Donatists. He confiscated Heraclianus' possessions and bestowed them on the military leader Constantius. Those Circumcellions who were captured were sent as colonists into the remote depths of Africa.

All this while Augustine continued to urge clemency and begged the imperial representatives to soften the coercive measures against the Donatists.

At this same time another attempt to seize Africa was made by Wallia, a king elected by the Visigoths. His plan was to approach the continent through the Strait of Gibraltar. "He who possesses Africa," he said, "possesses Rome, possesses Italy, possesses the Empire." But he failed, made his submission, and returned to allegiance to the emperor.

After putting down all these usurpers, Honorius celebrated his victory in Rome. Wallia was sent as an ally at the head of his Visigoths into Spain. However, he was repulsed and installed himself in Aquitaine and Narbonne, where he was granted a special status. Half of the revenues from Roman property in the zone he occupied was turned over to him. The Visigoths retained their national autonomy and paid no taxes to Rome (the idea of taxation, they said, was incompatible with their concept of liberty). The emperor granted complete amnesty to any of his subjects who had committed a crime in order to save his life when it was threatened by the barbarians. Henceforth, in Africa as in Gaul, the functionaries would be natives of the region.

That same year of 413 the tribune Marcellinus was accused of having plotted with Heraclianus to separate Africa from the Empire. This accusation was the revenge of the Donatists, abetted by Count Marinus. Marcellinus was arrested, prosecuted and condemned.

Augustine went immediately to Carthage to visit Marcellinus in prison, and questioned him at length. He was deeply moved at Marcellinus' dignified demeanor in his dungeon. "The darkness of the deepest dungeon," he wrote, "can in no way approach the horror of the black revenge that reigns in the hearts of the wicked."

Count Marinus determined to have Marcellinus executed at once, despite the efforts of Augustine, who felt obliged to leave a city "where so great an evil was being committed." It was not long, however, before Count Marinus himself was punished. In the course of the year 414, a former pretorian prefect, Nichomacus Flavianus, was sent to Africa to restore order, for the province had been in a state of turmoil ever since Heraclianus' sedition. Marinus, convicted of extortions and abuse of power, was deported.

It had taken Alaric's sack of Rome to bring Augustine to begin the writing of the first history of religion, his *City of God*. It took the schism of Pelagius for him to formulate his doctrine of grace and to finish his book *On the Trinity*.

Pelagius, a monk of Britain, objected to the Christian concept of original sin. According to him, men were not submitted to punishment for the fault of their first parents, Adam and Eve. They could themselves choose, by their own free will, between good and evil, and of their own accord live sinless lives.

Pelagianism met at once with the most violent opposition from the Fathers of the Church, Jerome and Augustine. For Augustine, the whole body of Christian doctrine rested on the *transmission of original sin* and *man's predestination*. We have seen him at grips with Manichaeism, which dealt with the nature of God, the Creation of the world and the origin of evil—questions which have tormented the minds of countless men. Then he fought Donatism, a purely local schism, which involved the principle of the universality of the Church. Before he would leave the world he would strike his blow against Arianism, which denies the divinity of Christ. But prior to this, he waged a battle against Pelagianism for twenty years.

His first book concerning this heresy was his tract *On the Punishment and Remission of Sin*. In this he explained that without supernatural aid our will is powerless to triumph over evil desires. A tendency to evil resides within our flesh not because it was instilled there by the Creator but as the consequence of Adam's fall. Augustine recognized that man, through his free will and God's grace, could refrain from sin, but this happened only rarely. It is God's grace which reveals to us those things which our own infirmities hide from our eyes.[2]

Thus Augustine laid the foundations of the doctrine of grace, namely that all will to do good is God's gift, and that each of our good works is inspired by God. This doctrine of grace came from St. Paul, who said: "What hast thou that thou hast not received? And if thou hast received it, why dost thou boast as if thou had not received it?"

The enemies of the Church's teaching ask: "If bodily death came to us because of sin, then why did men continue to die after the Redeemer has granted us the remission of sin?"

Augustine replied that man was condemned to eat his bread in the sweat of his brow, and woman to bring forth children in groaning—could we not equally ask why these things continue to be? He said that before the Redemption, pain had been the punishment of sinners, but it was now the struggle and trial of the just. As for death, it is for us "the occasion of a glorious combat."

However, since in the East men always seem to have been somewhat indifferent to the problem of man's free will, Pelagius was successful in having his teachings accepted by two synods (in 415). On the other hand, in 416, Pelagianism was condemned by two African synods; and in 417, Pope Innocent I confirmed this condemnation. But his sentence was rescinded that same year by his successor Zosimus, who was tricked into belief in Pelagius' orthodoxy.

Augustine made desperate efforts to enlighten Zosimus, even to the point of declaring he was ready to renounce his bishopric if his efforts were unavailing.

In the month of November 417, in Carthage, a council of two hundred and forty bishops upheld their initial decree and declared: "We have ordered that the sentence against Pelagius and Celestius (his friend and follower) remain as we have pronounced, and make a clear confession of our belief that God's grace, through Jesus Christ, Our Lord, aids us not only to know but to do what is right, and that without this grace we can neither say nor do anything which is truly virtuous."

The Pope replied that matters should be left as they stood, but Augustine's influence was considerable. He wrote to the emperor to explain the problem clearly, and Honorius decreed, on April 30, 418, that Pelagius and Celestius should be expelled from Rome and that those who followed their teaching should be subject to confiscation of property and to deportation. Another synod meeting at Carthage again confirmed the ecclesiastical condemnation of Pelagianism and its adherents. Then Pope Zosimus also modified his position and condemned the doctrines of Pelagius and Celestius. (They were later condemned in the East at the Council of Ephesus, in 431.)

The time now seemed ripe for Augustine to resume his work *On the Trinity*, which he "began when he was young and finished in old age."

In the first two books, he sets out to prove, by means of Holy Scripture, the unity and equality of the Three Persons of the Trinity—which does not prevent the procession of the Son and the Holy Spirit from the Father. In Book IV, he deals with the mission of the Son. In Books VI and VII, he gives proofs of the unique nature of Divine Power and Wisdom, as also of the unique nature of the Three Persons.

These Three Persons are but one God, and this is incomprehensible to man's unaided reason:

"Let us believe then, with a firm filial devotion, in one God, Father, Son and Holy Spirit, in such a way that we do not believe the Son to be the Father, nor the Father to be the Son, nor either of them to be the Spirit of them both. Let there be no thought of anything being separated in this Trinity by time or place, but let us realize that these Three Things are equal and coeternal, and are absolutely one nature. We must not suppose that one part of creation was made by the Father, part by the Son, part by the Holy Spirit, but that all things and sundry that have been or are being created subsist by the whole Trinity's creation. In the same way no one is saved or redeemed by the Father without the Son and the Holy Spirit, or by the Son without the Father and the Holy Spirit, or by the Holy Spirit without the Father and the Son, but by the Father and the Son and the Holy Spirit."

The fifth part of the work is a reply to the Arians who attacked the mystery of the Trinity by trying to prove a difference in *substance* between the Father and the Son.

The work ends with a most beautiful prayer:

"O Lord my God, my one hope, listen to me, do not let me give up seeking You for weariness, let me eagerly seek Your face always.

"Give me the strength to seek, since You have let Yourself be found, and have given us the hope of finding You more and more. You have before You my strength and my weakness; preserve the one, heal the other. You have before You my knowledge and my ignorance; receive me as I enter the door You have opened to me, open to me as I knock at the door You have closed to me. May I remember You, understand

You, love You. Increase in me these three things, until You refashion me to perfection."

Augustine also finished his book *On Genesis*, "a work," he said later in his *Retractations*, "which sought the truth rather than finding it."

Around this time there occurred an event that was to have incalculable consequences: Count Boniface was appointed governor of Africa. He had been the defender of Masilia (Marseille) against the Goths in 413, and was famous everywhere for his ability and bravery. Ties, first of respect, then of friendship, bound him to Augustine.

We may mention in passing that at this period indifference to faith was inadmissible. Insofar as he was able, Augustine had opposed the death penalty for heretics, but it now seemed to him that force might be necessary to achieve unity. "At the marriage feast described in the Gospel parable," he said, "the words, 'Compel them to enter,' were not used until the first invitations had gone unheeded."

Boniface was of like mind and consulted him on all occasions. The death of his wife had plunged him into despair, and in a famous letter written in 418, Augustine told him (at a time when Boniface seems to have wanted to leave the life of the world and enter a monastery) that a man could gain salvation as a soldier; Rome and the Church had need of him for their defense.

"When you arm yourself for combat," Augustine said, "arm yourself also with the thought that even your bodily strength is a gift from God. When you make a promise, you must keep faith, even with an enemy. Although you may be forced into war, you must always desire peace, so that God may deliver us from the necessity of war. War should be made only that peace may be obtained. If you must take the life of an enemy in battle let it be by necessity and not by your will. In the same way, you should show mercy toward a vanquished enemy."

Meanwhile, the day of reckoning was drawing near. Men

were stricken with terror by the eclipse of the sun on July 19, 418. There were violent earthquakes, especially in Palestine and Languedoc. Was the end of the world at hand? Augustine did not think so.

"Before the Lord," he said, "a thousand years are as one day, and He surely does not will to limit the duration of mankind to only a few centuries after the coming of His Son to earth."

How with all these things—the writing of his philosophical books, the direction of his diocese, the sermons he gave several times a week—did Augustine find time to found monasteries? Nevertheless, he is the father of monastic life in Africa, and in addition to the communities at Hippo, established many others on African soil. He carefully drew up the rule of his order—a model of monastic regulation which passed over the seas and down through the ages. More than fifty religious orders have been established in accordance with Augustine's rule.

The year 418 was also the date of his journey to Caesarea (now Cherchel, fifty miles from Algiers) in Mauretania, where he preached against the Donatist bishop Emeritus. On his arrival he was welcomed with such enthusiasm that he had to speak in the public square, where the subject of his sermon was Catholic unity. On learning that the Caesareans had suddenly embraced the Catholic religion, the Donatist faction started a battle between citizens in the street. Nevertheless, on September 20, 418, before returning to Hippo, Augustine had consecrated a new church in Caesarea.

Chapter Ten

THE LAST YEARS
426–430

Roman Africa was fast approaching its end; the same would soon be true of Rome itself and of the Empire. The Goths, the Alans and the Vandals, after devastating Gaul and Spain, were preparing to cross the Mediterranean, and at the same time were following Alaric's pattern in assaults against Italy.

Now these barbarians were Arians, and in the event of their triumph it seemed certain that Catholicism would be wiped from the face of Africa. Augustine, who had dreamed of unifying Christ's earthly empire, knew hours of anxiety and anguish.

His attacks on Pelagianism became more violent; perhaps his obsession with the barbarian threat had something to do with his fury. This man, usually so moderate, undertook a pitiless attack on heresy, showing the utmost severity in his writings against such enemies of Christ as the Arians and Pelagians.

Nor was this all. Neither the Circumcellions nor the Donatists had been eradicated, and encouraged by the Empire's weakness, they had come out of hiding and served as the forerunners of the great tidal wave of barbarians. Moorish rebels from the Atlas Mountains and nomads from the south killed and burned all they met in their path. "This country in other days so prosperous and populous," wrote Augustine, "has fast been turned into a desert."

Even so, had Augustine paused to glance back at the whole of his life's work, he might have considered it near completion. The Manichaeans had been vanquished before God and man, the Donatists convicted of error and bad faith and many of their numbers brought back into the fold of the Church; the Pelagians had first been condemned at Carthage and this condemnation upheld by authority he personally brought to bear; Christian Africa was renowned throughout the world because of his prestige; and, due to his leadership, the Church of Africa had become a beacon of the faith. He could have prided himself on all these things, but, alas, this illustrious old man was fated to see his fatherland delivered over to the barbarians, and worse still, to see one of his friends, a great military chief, open the door to them.

The Emperor Honorius had not remarried after the death of his wife—Stilicho's daughter whom he had repudiated. On the other hand, his brother-in-law Constantius had a son, Flavius Valentinian. Constantius, who was now consul for the third time, was made Augustus on February 8, 421, and young Valentinian was named prince imperial. Theodosius II and the Eastern court made known their disapproval of this promotion, and after Constantius' death, Honorius became more and more solitary and distraught. He died in his turn at thirty-nine years of age. In principle his death left Emperor Theodosius II in Constantinople the sole ruler of the Empire; in fact, it led to a new outbreak of civil war.

Theodosius II had no intention of helping young Valentinian to reign over the West, and reached an understanding with Castin, the master of militia assigned to the consulate of the West. In Africa, Boniface supported the claims of little Valentinian and his mother Placidia, even trying to starve Italy anew by blockading the transport of grain. It thus became necessary either to crush Boniface or to give in and crown Valentinian. In opposition to Boniface, Rome in its turn proclaimed as emperor of the West the usurper Johannes, who immediately dispatched troops to Africa.

At this point the government in Constantinople altered its stand and suddenly restored to Placidia and Valentinian their status and dignity as Augusta and heir to the throne. Valentinian was proclaimed Caesar and the barbarian Ardabur was placed at the head of the Eastern armies to put down the usurper Johannes.

The latter sent to the Danube a functionary of his court, Aetius, to secure the help of the Hun allies. (Aetius had once been taken as a hostage by the Huns and has since been on friendly terms with them.) A part of the Eastern army marched into Italy, but its leader, Ardabur, fell into Johannes' hands. The usurper tried to negotiate a friendly arrangement but was betrayed by his soldiers and taken prisoner. He was sent to the court of Ravenna where, at Placidia's order, his hands were cut off. He was paraded before the populace in the circus and finally executed. Three days later, Aetius arrived at the head of his sixty thousand Huns! A truce was subsequently reached between him and the Augusta Placidia, and Aetius was commissioned to go into Gaul to fight the Visigoths who had approached dangerously near the Mediterranean coast.

Boniface had vanquished without difficulty the army sent against him by Johannes and was still in command of Africa. Valentinian III was made Augustus for the West at Rome, on October 23, 425. (We may note that at this same time a Hun empire was forming in central Europe, with Attila as its chief.)

Following this, Aetius, who had won the favor of the Augusta Placidia, decided to do away with Boniface, the African governor, whose influence he saw as a threat. He represented him to the Augusta as a secret enemy, especially since the Count of Africa had married an Arian. Placidia recalled Boniface to Ravenna but, at the same time, Aetius sent him a warning not to obey the Augusta's orders because his recall concealed a "horrible trap."

Boniface therefore remained in Carthage, which enabled

Aetius to convince Placidia that the Count of Africa had rebelled. Soon Boniface, seeing he would be attacked by massive forces if he did not give in, worked up a bitter resent-
ment against the imperial authority. He therefore turned for
help to the barbarians, those "instruments" of all vengeance,
human and divine.

Augustine was now sixty-five and was scarcely able to walk,
and he scarcely slept at all because of rheumatic pain. He
decided he must have the help of a coadjutor and on September 24, 426, in the course of a sermon declared:

"I know that after the death of bishops, the churches are
often troubled by rival ambitions and disputes. This is the
reason I now declare before you all my will: I designate as
my successor the priest Heraclius. I love his wisdom and I
spare his modesty my praise. When I ask you to allow him to
succeed me, I know that you desire him as well."

On this same occasion Augustine reminded his people that
they had promised to allow him to work in peace for four days
each week. He begged them therefore to address all inquiries
or requests concerning daily details to his coadjutor Heraclius.
He heard sounds of acclamation throughout the basilica and
was satisfied—Heraclius would succeed him. As for himself,
he would be able to finish his work *On Christian Doctrine*
which, with the *Confessions* and the *City of God* would
constitute the greatest trilogy of his writings.

As clouds gathered in the skies, and beneath the earth bur-
rowed those subterranean forces that would bring about the
Empire's collapse, the bishop of Hippo published in quick succession the last books of *On Christian Doctrine* and the final
part of the *City of God*.

The first part of *On Christian Doctrine* was an explanation
of the Scriptures. The second showed in what way divine
Truth should be understood.

Jesus wished for souls, by means of penance, to awaken to a
better life. As the love of God and love of neighbor are the

purpose envisaged by the Law and the aim of the Scriptures, this double precept should be applied to the understanding of the Bible texts—faith, hope, and charity are the three attributes that serve as a basis for the interpretation of the Holy Books.

Augustine added that the Holy Books, translated in olden times, are not always clearly understandable. He enumerated the procedures by which one may arrive at their perfect comprehension. It is necessary to guard against the literal interpretation of figurative expressions. He condemned those who are "slaves to the letter."

In the fourth part he deals with rhetoric, not that he desired to teach the precepts of eloquence for their own sake, because, he said, unless accompanied by Wisdom they were useless.[1] Christian eloquence is totally different from the eloquence of the profane schools; its object, its end, is supernatural. The sacred orator has no other purpose than to give birth to souls for Christ. He may not count on his own efforts for his teaching to bear fruit; he is but an agent of transmission, a "sower of the word of God."

Now too the *City of God* was finished. It was the encyclopedia of the fifth century, the Christian poem on man's destiny in its relationship to his origin and his final end. It "brings to a close the pagan world with its fables and philosophy" and Christianity is set in opposition to the gods of the old universe and the kings of human thought. Augustine shows the first as powerless to sustain the peoples who worshiped them, the second as trying to reach Truth with no other wings than the powers of the human mind. But virtue is the gift of God, and we may neither hope for virtue unless it pleases God to help us, nor for happiness unless it pleases Him to lead us to find our happiness in Him.

"The God we worship chose certain spirits and gave them the power of foresight, and through them He makes prophecies. To others He gave the gift of healing. He controls the beginnings, progress and endings of wars when they are needed for the punishment or reformation of mankind. He rules the universal element of fire, so vehement and violent, yet so necessary for the equilibrium of nature. He is the Creator and Ruler of all the water of the universe. He made the sun, the brightest of all luminous bodies, and He gave it an appropriate energy and motion.

"His sovereignty and power reach to the lowest things. All that grows and sustains animal life, He produced and made appropriate for different natures. He gave us the earth, the fertility of soil, and foods for man and beast. All causes, primary and secondary, come within His knowledge and control. He gave to the moon its phases, and in the air and on the ground he provided means of traveling. He endowed the human intelligences which He created with a knowledge of the arts and sciences which help both life and nature. He instituted mating and marriage for the propagation of life. . . .

"The truth is that all these actions and energies belong to the one true God, who is really a God, who is wholly present everywhere, is confined by no frontiers and bound by no hindrances, is indivisible and immutable, and, through His nature has no need either of heaven or earth. He fills them both with His presence and His power."

The bishop of Hippo had reached the end of his work. This is the reason he now undertook a sort of criticism of his own books which he embodied in the *Retractations*. He wished to recapitulate and submit to scrutiny all that he had written before he arrived at the gates of death. Tormented by scruples, this great man reviewed, book by book, the whole of his writings. In this way he struggled against any pride he might have felt in his achievements. He labored without surcease at this revision because he wished to leave all he had written in good order.

The first volume of the *Retractations* includes the titles and study of all his writings from the time of his conversion until he became a bishop. The second analyzes those he wrote subsequently. This catalog lists two hundred and thirty-two books."

To his friend Quodvultdeus he addressed an analysis of "eighty-eight heresies," from Simon Magus down to the Pelagians, describing their origins and including a short criticism of the teachings of each. He spoke also of the question of the Jews,[2] and dictated a book on the *Predestination of the Saints*.

He had just finished the *Retractations* when he learned that Count Boniface, embittered by the attitude of the Augusta which was fostered, as we know, by the intriguer Aetius, had decided to call in the help of the Vandals.

Partly from anger and partly from fear, Boniface sent to Gonderic, the king of the Vandals, who was encamped in Spain, a trusted messenger charged with an offer to hand over to him, in return for his aid, a third of the Roman possessions in Africa. Gonderic's death placed Genseric, his son, at the head of the Vandal army (mixed with Goths and Alans), estimated as numbering eighty thousand fighters. Through the Strait of Gibraltar they passed from Spain into Africa in May 428, Boniface having placed at their disposition a large part of his navy.

With the support of the Circumcellions, who profited from this occasion to sap the Roman strength, the Vandals spread along the coast, continuing as far as the mountains of Mauretania.

The elderly Augustine, crippled by rheumatism, was no longer able to leave his cell. His voice had become so weak that he had been forced to give up preaching. He wrote to Boniface, with whom he had broken all ties since the latter's marriage to an Arian, recalling their past friendship, the plea for purity his first wife had made him on her deathbed and which had led him at one time to wish to become a monk. He thought Boniface would listen to the voice of his friend even if this voice were raised in blame.

"Your daughter has been baptized in the Arian heresy. You dishonor yourself with concubines. Nevertheless you are a

Christian and must fear God. Think on all the other things you have done which I do not care to mention. You will see for what grievous faults you should do penance."

After depicting Africa in the clutches of the barbarians, he went on: "Who would have thought that under Boniface, the Count of Africa and the hero of imperial wars, who when but a simple tribune imposed peace between nations by force of arms, who would have thought that under him the barbarians would strike far into the provinces and spread such ravages, such ruin? On every side it was said that so long as the Count of Africa was in power, the barbarians would be repelled. Alas, these hopes have been confounded!"

Augustine brutally touched on the most sensitive point, for he felt he must cut to the quick:

"Ponder on those accounts you must settle with God. Turn your thoughts to Christ, who did so much that was good and suffered so much that was evil. If you have received much that is good from the Empire, do not render it evil for good. And if you have received evil from it, do not render evil for evil.

"You say you have just reasons for your action? I am not the judge, but can you affirm before God that you would have arrived at this point if you had not loved earthly possessions, possessions which, as a servant of God, you should hold in contempt?

"What shall I say of Africa's devastation by the barbarians which is met by no resistance? You do nothing to prevent this calamity! Who could have believed such a thing! They ravage, pillage, change into a desert this prosperous and populous land. Not even a single fruit tree remains standing.

"But, you reply, these things should be blamed on those who have offended you, those who have repaid your loyalty with bitter enmity. Such reasons as these I do not accept. All you have to fear is offending Christ Himself."

Augustine then counseled Boniface to "find his former

soul," to do penance for the sins he had committed, to determine to renounce sin in the future.

At peril of his life, the priest Paul carried this letter to Carthage. But Boniface was committed to the rebellion he had begun—too proud to denounce it, too involved to withdraw.

The terrorized inhabitants cried loudly for baptism and did public penance for their sins. Augustine solemnly declared that the bishops and priests must not abandon their dioceses or churches; on the contrary, they must remain even when threatened by martyrdom. In doing so, they would have the consolation of assisting the dying in their last hours and of preventing the apostasies that occurred under the influence of fear. The people were fleeing, leaving behind hostages who were certain to be put to death—the old, the infirm, and the sick. What priest worthy of his name would abandon such as these?

Crowds of men and women of all ages pressed into the churches to be reconciled to God and to His ministers. "Religion and the fatherland," said Augustine, "will always have an inviolable refuge—the hearts of their children. The priests will strive to keep these hearts pure, to console those in distress, and to relight the divine flame of hope in these souls."

A delegation led by Alypius succeeded in reaching Ravenna and implored the Augusta to try to reach an understanding with Boniface, if there was still time. The Augusta consented and recalled Sigisvult, the Roman general who was fighting both Boniface and the Vandals. She restored Boniface's authority and his commission to defend Africa for the Empire.

The Vandals meanwhile continued their advance across Mauretania, committing unimaginable atrocities, and everywhere the Circumcellions opened up the way.

Count Darius, sent from Ravenna to negotiate with Boniface, arrived in Carthage. Augustine immediately addressed a letter to the imperial plenipotentiary in which he said: "You are sent by God to prevent the shedding of blood. Rejoice in this, illustrious and dear son in Jesus Christ. May God shower down His blessings on you for the good you have done."

To this Darius replied: "May you long live to formulate such wishes for the Empire and for the Republic of Rome."

Darius tried to reach a truce with the Vandals and was successful. But who could hope that, once having entered Africa, the barbarians would depart? The booty that had fallen into his hands was too fine for Genseric to agree to abandon it. Boniface led a last desperate battle and was defeated by overpowering numbers. He then took refuge in Hippo, soon to be cut off by land and blockaded by sea. Boniface and Augustine thus found themselves imprisoned in the city behind hastily constructed fortifications. Three cities still resisted the encroaching tide: Carthage, Hippo and Cirta.

The government in Ravenna was powerless to stem the advance of the Vandals, and Placidia begged help from Theodosius II.

Everywhere cities were burned, cultivated land laid waste, churches profaned, Christians killed and their corpses piled high in streams of blood. The Vandals destroyed monasteries, cemeteries and churches, lighting great bonfires to burn down the sacred places. Priests, virgins and monks were disemboweled. Bishops' mouths were opened with sticks and filled with mud by impious hands; they were made to swallow saltwater, vinegar, and lye. Burdened down like camels, they were yoked and made to walk like oxen, pricked from behind by iron lances. Several bishops were burned alive.

The mountains and forests served as refuges for the fugitives and there they died of starvation. The highways were filled with naked humans begging for alms. Soon desolation reigned from Tangiers to Tripoli.

Augustine was tormented by anguish, but he did not allow this to be seen. "He did not judge the invasion," said Possidius, "as it was judged by other men. Looking higher, he saw the peril to souls. The last days of his life he found bitter and sorrowful, yet he ever strove to lift up the courage of his people."

The correspondence he carried on during the last months of his life contains a series of letters written in a warlike vein and which must have expressed the feelings of Hippo's inhabitants as they watched the fiery night skies, reflecting the flames of the burning cities and villages around them.

When Bonifacc attcmptcd a sortic and drovc thc barbarians back, Augustine wrote to him: "Your Excellency is not unaware that I am confined to my bed where I await my last hour with longing. I rejoice at your victory. I abjure you to save the Roman city. Govern your soldiers as a good count. Do not presume on your own strength. Place your renown in the hands of Him who gives courage and you will have nothing to fear from any enemy whatsoever."

Until the end he preserved this proud attitude. He knew the Mediterranean should be a Roman lake and that the day the African coast was lost to the Empire, the Empire would bc lost as well.

He continued to work on his refutation of Julian of Eclanum's eight books in defense of Pelagius. He expressed himself briefly and precisely, for he felt more pressed than ever, knowing he was "very close to the mysteries."

He had finished the sixth book of his reply to Julian when illness again forced him to take to his bed. The time was approaching when the lamp of his life would be extinguished, yet he was not allowed to remain undisturbed. A man brought a sick person to him, asking him to effect a cure. Shaking with fever, Augustine replied: "Had I some power over sickness, I would begin by curing myself."

But the man told of a dream in which a voice had said to him: "Go out and find Augustine. He will lay his hand on your sick friend, and he will be cured." This indeed happened, and it was the only miracle performed by the saint during his lifetime.

Finally he persuaded others to leave him in peace. Only one

was allowed to remain at his bedside—Alypius, the brother of his heart since the time of their wild youth, who now arrived to rejoin Augustine since Tagaste, his own see city, had been destroyed.

Possidius tells us that Augustine had the Penitential Psalms copied and placed on the wall so he could read and reread them from his bed. It was while he lay on his deathbed that he received the visit of the messenger of Theodosius, emperor of the East, who requested the great Doctor to represent the Church of Africa at the Council that would open in Ephesus at Pentecost. Augustine declined this great honor with sadness in his heart.

Ten days before his death he asked his friends to leave him alone, and even Alypius no longer came into his room. Only the doctor entered from time to time and a brother who brought him the little food he was able to swallow.

"Even though they have been baptized, Christians and priests should never leave this life without having made a general examination of conscience," he said. Methodically he reviewed his past, passing over every detail of his long, full life. He thought of his struggles with himself and with others. Had he waged such battles so that barbarism might win? No, no, it was not the hour to make judgments, but to give oneself over to penance and obscurity.

He had done what he could during every day and every hour that he had carried on his enormous task. He had established a model church and monasteries, and had instructed the clergy. The results he had obtained were considerable—he had sown the good grain, and it was ready to spring forth. But now the barbarian invasion threatened the destruction of all his work.

"In the old man," writes Louis Bertrand, "he recognized the new, and he said: 'What! It is only myself. I have not changed, only found myself. From my youth, even in the midst of my errors, I was trying, my God, to turn to You.'

"His worst folly had been to try to understand everything;

humility of spirit had been lacking in him. Finally in the end, God had given him the grace to submit his intelligence to faith. He had believed, and *then* he had understood—as he could and as much as he could. He had made magnificent use of his reason, within the limitations assigned to mortal man. Was not the most ardent desire of his youth to comprehend?

"And also to love. After rooting out his earthly passions, he had made good use of his heart. Yes, to love, all was contained in this. Let the barbarians come, for had not Christ said, 'I will be with you until the consummation of the world?' So long as two men gathered together out of love for Him, the world could not be completely lost."

At his last hour he thought of his mother Monica, of his son Adeodatus and of the humble and self-sacrificing companion who awaited him in the world beyond.

On August 28, 430, prayers were said for him in all the churches of Hippo and especially in the Basilica of Peace where so much of his work had been carried on. Possidius, Alypius and two other bishops were singing canticles with him. Suddenly Augustine's thin, feeble voice could no longer be heard. He died in the midst of the song.

All Hippo trembled. In the midst of the misfortunes that surrounded them, their defender was no longer there to give the inhabitants lessons and examples of courage. He had left the Earthly City for the City of God.

Mankind was entering on the long night of barbarism. Augustine had lighted the lamp that would illuminate its passage.

Chapter Eleven

AFTERWARD

Saint Augustine died on August 28, 430. The siege of Hippo by the barbarian armies was to last until the summer of 431.

The regent Placidia having called Theodosius II to her aid, Eastern forces under Aspar landed in Africa. Genseric raised the siege of Hippo, but this was only a maneuver, for in 432 the Vandals became masters of all Roman Africa with the exception of Carthage and Cirta, which were still under siege.

The imperial government was all the more powerless to combat the Vandals because new troubles broke out in Italy itself. Aetius, Boniface's enemy, revolted against the Empire soon after his arrival in Gaul. Placidia recalled Boniface from Africa and made him general of the Roman armies. Boniface defeated Aetius, but in doing so, he met his death. Placidia thereupon appointed his son-in-law Sebastian as his successor.

Aetius, supported by the Huns, reentered Italy in 433. Now he was in a position to force the Augusta to restore him to his position as commander-in-chief of the imperial armies. Aetius' return led Genseric to decide to negotiate with the Empire. A treaty with the Vandals was concluded by Trigetius at Hippo on February 11, 435, in which these barbarians were recognized as "allies of the Empire," and allowed to retain possession of a part of Mauretania, of Numidia and the northern corner of the proconsular province. Actually Genseric's acceptance of these terms was only a pretense; he was merely awaiting the opportunity to take over the whole of Roman Africa.

During this final collapse of the Empire, traitorous generals everywhere called in the barbarians to support them in the attainment of their personal ambitions.[1] The Visigoths arrived on the Mediterranean coast of Gaul and besieged Narbonne. The Huns too invaded Gaul but were defeated near Toulouse. Weakened by these battles, the Visigoths signed a treaty with Rome in 439 and were thenceforth recognized as "a sovereign people."

That same year, on October 19, Genseric took Carthage, and became master of the whole province of Africa. Romans and the Catholic Church were despoiled of all they possessed; those of senatorial rank, Roman citizens and members of the clergy were sold as slaves, and the churches of Carthage given over to the Arian clergy.

Genseric then built up a powerful navy, its base the port of Carthage, and thus made himself the master of the Mediterranean Sea. The Western government nevertheless made an effort to defend Naples under the leadership of the general Sigisvult. The Vandals landed in Sicily in June 440, despoiling and persecuting the Catholics, but remained unsuccessful in their efforts to penetrate into Italy.

A compromise peace treaty was signed in 442, dividing Africa in such a way as to leave to the Empire only Mauretania, Numidia, and Tripoli. The Vandal king was recognized as the "sovereign prince," and this precarious arrangement continued until the death of Valentinian III in 445. The lands were given over entirely to the Vandals, and domains formerly belonging to the Romans became "royal" property.

When certain Catholics refused to be converted to Arianism, Genseric had them executed. Numerous Africans, deprived of all their possessions, fled to Italy, where the exiles received lands and tax exemption for life.

The imperial government then tried to aid in the ecclesias-

tical organization of the West. Under the pontificate of Pope
Leo the Great, the Church endeavored to save the civilization
that survived.

Meanwhile the Burgundians took over Gaul and divided the
land among themselves. The Visigoths were definitely established in Aquitaine, and the Alans occupied the region of
Valence, while other among them occupied the banks of the
Loire. In 451, Attila crossed the Rhine, sacked on April 7
the city of Metz and descended as far south as Orléans.

Italy was in a state of such frightful misery that, it is told,
parents sold their children into slavery. Then the Visigoths,
uneasy about the future of their kingdom, made an alliance
with Rome against Attila. This Hun chieftain was defeated
in Champagne in the famous struggle known in history as the
Battle of Châlons, 451, after which Attila led his decimated
army back across the Rhine.

The finances of the Empire were in a dreadful condition.
The priest Salvianus wrote a violent book called *On the Government of God* (*De Gubernatione Dei*) in which he exclaimed: "What folly to believe that personal wealth can be
retained if the State is poor and destitute!"[2]

The Emperor Valentinian personally liquidated Aetius by
a blow from his sword—together with several of his ministers
and courtesans, whose dead bodies were exposed in the Forum
during a ceremony in which the Emperor appeared to deliver
a solemn allocution. The eunuch Heraclius headed the new
government, but the news of the death of the famous general
Aetius had excited the barbarians, and the Franks again
crossed the Rhine. The Alamans appeared to establish themselves in Switzerland and the Saxons pillaged the Channel
coasts.

On March 16, 455, the emperor was stabbed to death by
one of Aetius' friends. With Valentinian III, grandson of
Theodosius the Great, came to an end the dynasty that had
occupied the Roman throne for ninety-one years.

After the assassination of Valentinian III, Petronius Maxi-

mus was proclaimed emperor on March 17, 455. To strengthen
and legitimize his position he married the dead emperor's
widow, Eudoxia.

Genseric took action at once, and in May the Vandal navy
cast anchor at the mouth of the Tiber. The troops that landed
were made up of Vandals and also of Moors and former Circumcellions. Panic spread throughout Rome, and after being
abandoned by his guards the emperor was forced to flee. In
the course of this flight he was stoned to death by a furious
mob, on May 31, 455. Genseric made his entrance into the
Eternal City on June 2.

For weeks Rome was given over to pillage by the Vandals
and the Moors. Genseric sent back to Africa the art treasures
of the ancient world which had accumulated in Rome over the
centuries. When he left the city on June 16 to return to Carthage, he led with him into captivity several thousand
Roman citizens, including senators who had not fled in time,
and the Empress Eudoxia. The Vandal king then brought
under submission those regions of Africa which the treaty of
442 had reserved to the Empire.

In 456, Genseric sent out a flotilla of sixty vessels to beset
the Empire anew, but the imperial government was successful in repulsing this attack.

Although Gaul definitely abandoned the Empire at this
time, the Roman general Majorinus was proclaimed emperor
by his soldiers, on April 1, 457. He immediately began the
building of a number of ships to guard the Western Empire
against its enemies and to reconquer the Mediterranean, now
completely in the power of the barbarians. He strengthened
the army, renewed relations with the Gauls, and was praised
in Lyon by the poet Sidonius Apollinaris, a repentant former
rebel. He concluded a treaty with the Burgundians, and massed
troops in Sicily to protect the island from Vandal attack.
The Vandals, however, surprised the Roman navy on the
Spanish coast and succeeded in its capture. The emperor was

obliged to cede not only all Africa to Genseric but also the Balearic Islands, Sardinia and Corsica.

The Visigoths in the south and the Burgundians in the north became completely independent of the Empire. Moreover, the Vandals made constant assaults on the defenses of Sicily and southern Italy. A last Roman expedition against the Vandals ended in failure, despite an initial successful landing at Cape Bon near Carthage.

Finally, on October 31, 475, young Romulus Augustulus was made emperor of the Empire, but an empire reduced to a very small amount of territory. Completely ruined, it could no longer fulfill its engagements to its army, whereupon the troops elected as their head the son of the last king of the Heruli, Odoacer, a Germanic leader. He was proclaimed emperor on August 23, 476, and deposed young Romulus Augustulus although he spared his life.

Forty-six years after Saint Augustine's death, thirty-seven years after the fall of Carthage, the Roman Empire of the West disappeared from the map of the world. The Arab invasion of Africa, two and a half centuries later, wiped out all that remained of the famous African Church.

In 710, Saint Fulgence succeeded in removing Saint Augustine's body from the church of Saint Stephen in Hippo in order to save it from Mussulman desecration. He had it transported to Sardinia, where Pope Gregory II was able to ransom it from the Saracens and bring it to the church of Saint Peter in Pavia.

A fiery temperament, an unrivaled intellect, a searcher who reached the farthest limits a man can hope to attain, a lover of truth who investigated everything, a man of such power to convince that he converted all those who followed him—such was Saint Augustine.[3]

He plumbed to the depths of more subjects than had any other Father of the Church, threw more light on the Christian dogmas than any other before his time, and mounted to the higher meaning of these teachings "with a power that will never cease to astonish men." His life was one long spiritual combat, a combat of the soul, a combat of the Christian against all the enemies of the Church and of the Empire.

"His century," Louis Bertrand wrote (forty years ago), "was very similar to our own. He came into a declining world, a world on the brink of a great cataclysm which would engulf a whole civilization, a tragic turn in history which must have been difficult to live through and have appeared hopeless to even the staunchest of spirits."

Manichaeism denatured the divine Essence and denatured man as well. Saint Augustine enabled men to understand that evil is not a substance but the absence of good, that Creation is good, that evil is the work of the human will and not the work of God. Thus he restored to man the knowledge that he was free, and to God a comprehension on man's part of His unity and His goodness.

In a ceaseless struggle in the defense of the Catholic faith, he fought and conquered the errors that tended to divide the universal Church. He demolished Donatism and Pelagianism with a clarion appeal to man's reason. Due to his ardent desire to always comprehend, he found a true place for the genius of the West in the development of the Christian faith.

The first of the theologians, he remains the first of Christian philosophers.

"What, then, is time?" he said in his *Confessions:* "If no one asks me, I know; if I want to explain it to one who does ask me, I do not know. Yet I state confidently that I know this: if nothing were passing away, there would be no past time, and if nothing were coming, there would be no future time, and if nothing existed, there would be no present time.

"How, then, can these two kinds of time, the past and the future, be, when the past no longer is and the future as yet does not be? But if the present were always present, and would not pass into the past, it would no longer be time but eternity. . . . If any point of time is conceived that can no

longer be divided into even the most minute parts of a moment, that alone it is which may be called the present. It
flies with such speed from the future into the past that it
cannot be extended by even a trifling amount. For if it is extended, it is divided into past and future. The present has no
space. . . . For this reason it seems to me that time is nothing more than a distention: but of what thing I know not, and
the marvel is, if it is not of the mind itself."

For him, reason united to faith is the only *noble way* to
believe. But also, no one listened more intently than he to
the soul's counsel to rise toward faith.

For fifteen centuries Saint Augustine has dominated as a
theologian and a philosopher. He is also for us a deeply human
example, for he knew error, temptation and suffering.[4] What
stands out in his writings is an infinite love for God. He loved
to the point of folly. "The measure for loving God is God
Himself. The measure for this love is to love without measure."

He knew that of himself man can do nothing; he can neither bring himself happiness, nor win faith, nor acquire virtue.
Nevertheless he knew it was by faith, virtue and perseverance
that beatitude is gained.

"It was pride," he wrote, "that caused the fall of Lucifer
and Adam. If you should ask me what are the ways to God,
I would tell you that the first is humility, the second is humility, and the third is still humility. Not that there are no
other precepts to give, but if humility does not precede all
that we do, our efforts are fruitless."

His work is made up of a surprising juxtaposition of op-
posites from which the truth springs forth as though by inter-
action. He turned everything into account—his sensuality he
changed into a yearning for things divine, his taste for enjoyment into peace, his human love into Christian charity.

"We are the temples of God," he said, "all of us together
and each one of us in particular, since He deigns to dwell
within the soul of each one of the faithful as well as in the

body of the Church; nor is He greater in all than in each, because extent and division are repellent to him."

Yes, and we must not forget that despite the rigor and severity of the barriers he set up to guard his own conduct, he is a poet of love.

"The only true virtue," he said, "is that which stems from love. Some men practice apparent virtue because they fear punishment. He who refrains from sin out of fear of chastisement is an enemy of justice."

He was the forerunner and embodiment of all the great Doctors of Christianity. Gregory the Great, Anselm, Abelard, Albertus Magnus, Saint Bernard, Saint Thomas and Descartes were his direct posterity.

He brought preciseness to the doctrinal definitions of Catholicism. He is truly our spiritual father, and "he taught us the language of prayer."

He was also an African. More than any other writer he expressed the genius of his country—that African mixture of passion, contradiction, violence, gravity, mobility, reality and fantasy.

For us Christians today, it is a grave thought that the mouthpiece of Catholicism, the witness of the fall of the Roman Empire, was a man of that century and of that continent—Augustine, the greatest of all Africans.

CHRONOLOGY

332 Birth of Saint Monica, Augustine's mother

345 New uprising of the Circumcellions in alliance with the Donatists

354 November 13. Birth of Saint Augustine at Tagaste

364 Final separation of the two Roman Empires

374 Firmus the Moor supported by the Donatists. General Theodosius before the walls of Tipasa. Saint Ambrose, bishop of Milan

375 Saint Augustine returns to Tagaste from Carthage (21 years of age)

378 Edict of Valentinian I against the Manichaeans

379 Valentinian dies. Gratian associates Theodosius with him on the imperial throne. Valentinian II made emperor

380 Theodosius closes the Arian churches

381 The Council of Constantinople completes the Nicene creed and condemns the heretics.

383 Saint Augustine in Rome. Abandons the Manichaeans (at 29 years of age). Gratian dies. Maximus proclaims himself emperor. Symmachus, prefect of Rome, opposed by Theodosius

384 Saint Augustine in Milan

385 Delivers oration in praise of Theodosius

386 Retreat at Cassiciacum (*Against the Academics, On Order, On the Happy Life*)

387 Massacre at Thessalonica. Saint Augustine's conversion. (*On the Immortality of the Soul, The Soliloquies.*) Baptized by Saint Ambrose at Milan (April 24). Leaves for Africa. Saint Monica dies at Ostia (No-

NOTES

Chapter One

1 Tertullian was born A.D. 160 and died at Carthage in 230. He was the son of a Roman centurion who served as proconsul in Africa. Like other young men who wished to make their mark in a liberal career, Tertullian learned Greek and studied law, later attaining renown as an advocate. His parents were pagan and he himself did not become a Christian until he reached his middle years.

Cyprian, bishop of Carthage, who brought order and discipline to the Church of North Africa, was beheaded September 14, 258. At the same time in Cirta (Constantine) many others were martyred for the Christian faith—Maira, James, Rusticus, etc.

2 "Despite his power and the honor still paid him as a god, the reigning Roman emperor was, from the constitutional point of view, only an elected magistrate. His dignity was not hereditary. The vacancy of the throne was filled through the cooperation of the army, the Senate, and the people. During the last two centuries of the Empire, the people's participation in the imperial election was limited to the reading of the Senate's decree to the Roman populace and its acclamation by them.

"The essential attributes of the imperial office were attached to the title of *Imperator*. In the days of the Republic, this title was reserved to a general who had led a victorious army against the enemy. As a result, up to the third century the army had the same rights as the Senate in the election of an emperor, and an election by the Senate was not valid until it received ratification by the army. In 282 the Emperor Carus failed to have his election by the troops confirmed by the Senate and thereby established a precedent that made the Senate's approval no longer necessary for the election of an emperor chosen by the army.

"The imperial power could be exercised simultaneously by two personages, or even more. If an emperor himself proposed it, a co-emperor could be appointed who, upon the death of the first emperor, automatically became the first ruler. The co-emperors were often young men to whom their fathers assured succession in this way, and they could be invested in office in childhood.

"The emperor had sole right to the high command of the army, and held supreme governmental authority over the whole Empire with the exception of Rome. He had the right to convoke the Senate, to preside over it, and to propose measures for adoption; he could also veto the decision of the Senate or the administrative measures of the senatorial magistrates, and could control membership in the Senate and in the equestrian orders. He had police powers, and presided over official pagan ceremonies. Finally he had legislative and judicial powers, and the right to appoint the magistrates of Roman municipalities.

"The emperor bore the names of Imperator, Caesar and Augustus. In these titles the word Augustus was placed after the personal name of the ruler, and the words Imperator and Caesar before it. The emperor's wives were given the title of Augusta and had various honorary rights.

"Certain men could obtain, as a preliminary step to the imperial dignity, the rank and title of Caesar, enabling them to participate in such imperial honors as the right to wear the purple robe."
ERNEST STEIN

[3] The desire of Constantine and his sons, Constantine II, Constantius II, and Constans I, for peace with the Arians was opposed by St. Athanasius, who succeeded Alexander to the see of Alexandria on June 8, 328. He refused to receive Arius, who was more or less repentant, back among the Alexandrian clergy, thus going against the wishes of Constantine and his court. Despite urgent appeals to the Emperor, the patriarch Athanasius was exiled to Trier, where he lived until Constantine's death in 337.

During his exile, Athanasius gained influence over Constantine II, who became ruler of Britain, Gaul and Spain, and after the death of Constantine the Great, he was able to return to Alexandria. In 338, Constantius II, ruler of Asia Minor, Syria and Egypt, restored Athanasius and the other exiled bishops to their churches, but Athanasius was soon removed a second time by an Arian synod that met at Antioch. Gregory of Cappadocia, an Arian, was installed as his successor in Alexandria in March 339, at the price of much disorder and bloodshed. Athanasius took refuge with Pope Julius I, who convoked a synod at the end of 340 which declared Athanasius' removal null and void. Several months later, in Antioch, on the occasion of the dedication of a church begun by Constantine the Great, a new synod met in the presence of Emperor Constantius II, who ratified a formula of "moderate Arianism." But Constans I, formerly ruler of Italy, middle Africa, and Illyricum, and now, on the death of Constantine II, emperor of the West, protested so vigorously that Constantius gave in, fearing a war with his brother. On October 31, 346, Athanasius made a triumphal entry into Alexandria. The Arians then split into two factions, one moderate and the other "radical." The moderate semi-Arians denied the "consubstantiality" of Christ with God the Father, but declared the Son *equal* to the Father. On the other hand, the "radical" faction affirmed that the two Persons were different in *substance*. Constans was murdered in 350 and within three years Constantius was sole ruler of the Empire.

During the night of February 8–9, 356, the church in Alexandria where Athanasius was celebrating the divine office was surrounded by fifty soldiers, but Athanasius succeeded in escaping. Constantius judged the moment had come to bring the Church's dogma into agreement with his Arian convictions. In 357 at Sirmium, his capital, a synod affirmed the *likeness* of God the Father and of Christ, "a likeness of every kind, in conformity with Holy Scripture." This formula immediately caused a division among the Arians, and any temporary advances they had made were wiped out by the events that followed: resumption of the war in Persia, Julian's proclamation as Augustus by his troops, leading to the revival of paganism, and finally Constantius' death. Constantius' successor, Julian, immediately recalled the Nicaean bishops from exile so that the quarrels of the Christians would lead to dissensions and revive paganism.

On August 3, 379, the Emperor Gratian and Ambrose, the new bishop of Milan, reaffirmed the absolute validity of the decisions reached at Nicaea. Theodosius, on his side, promulgated (February 28, 380) a law ordering all his subjects to profess the teaching of Nicaea, represented by the two first bishops of Christianity, Damasus of Rome and Peter of Alexandria (whom Athanasius had appointed as his successor); the only Catholic Christians were those in communion with these two prelates.

In May 381 there finally met at Constantinople an ecumenical council (convoked by Theodosius) which definitely confirmed the teaching of Nicaea.

On September 3, 381, a Western council called by Gratian assembled at Aquila under the spiritual direction of Ambrose. Here it was decided that the remaining Arian bishops were to be condemned and deposed if they persisted in their heresy.

However, the Arian heresy had reached the outskirts of the Empire and had spread particularly among the Goths and Visigoths with whom the emperors wished to be on good terms. Moreover, the Arian doctrine had strong supporters at court, and, as we shall see, particularly in the Empress Justine, mother of Valentinian.

Chapter Two

1 "At the end of the fourth century the knowledge of Greek was beginning to disappear from the West. Greek had become a foreign language and its literature was accessible only in translation, at that time considered purely a scholarly exercise. Augustine owed the knowledge of Greek philosophy which he obtained by reading Circero to the translations of the latter's works by Victorinus of Apuleia. 'What exists in Greek,' Augustine later said, 'is surely perfect, but it is difficult to find anyone who is able to read or understand the language.'" HENRI MARROU

2 "The new Carthage made one forget the old Carthage of the Phoenicians, and bowed its head only to Rome. The African authors bestowed on it their most lavish praise, and it is certain that the Roman capital of the province of Africa was no less important than the old metropolis of the Phoenicians. Almost as populous as Rome, it was equal to it in size. Before the Vandal invasion it had no walls and overflowed into the country with its gardens, villas and burying grounds, covering almost all of the now depopulated peninsula. It had its capital and its palatinate on the hill of Byrsa, where rose a temple dedicated to Jupiter, Juno and Minerva, not far from the great temple of Aesculapius, the embodiment of the old Punic god Eschmun." LOUIS BERTRAND

3 Mani, the founder of the Manichaean sect, was born in Persia at the beginning of the third century, and died around 274. He began life as a slave. His teaching was a mixture of ancient Eastern religions and Christianity. From the religion of Zoroaster he took the system of the two principles of Good and Evil, Light and Darkness. Manichaeism was to have a strong revival in the thirteenth century and in France ended with the Albigensians.

The Elect, or the Perfect, were the priests of this religion. In its original Persian form, Ormuz was the god of Good, and his reign was that of the Spirit; Zoroaster was his interpreter. Opposed to Ormuz was Ahriman, or the god of Evil, personifying the reign of

Matter. Science and materialism were Evil in the symbolic language of the East. Materialism and the Spirit therefore existed in perpetual dualism. The principle of Good strove always to win back what belonged to it.

⁴ A triple principle of the Manichaeans: the mouth, the hand, the womb. The *mouth* should utter no evil word nor eat any meat that was unclean—flesh was the Devil's invention. As for the *hand*, the Manichaeans opposed violence of any kind; they could not hunt game or even cut down a tree. They must live in peace with all nature. As for the *womb*, all carnal relations were evil; it was forbidden to procreate a child, since life on earth must be brought to an end as quickly as possible.

⁵ The title of "Pope" was not given to the Bishop of Rome until the third century. It was only in 1081 that Gregory VII had himself designated exclusively as "the Father of Christians" (at the Lateran Council).

However, by a decree of Valentinian III (445) the bishops of the West were officially placed under the jurisdiction of the Holy See in Rome. St. Cyprian addressed the Bishop of Rome as "the head of the Church" and the fountainhead of priestly unity. Gradually the unity of the Church was achieved under the aegis of St. Peter's See. The wave of barbarian invasions in the fifth century gave still more power and spiritual authority to the Bishop of Rome who guided the ship through the storms. Thus almost imperceptibly the temporal government of the emperor passed to the spiritual government of the Church.

The following is a list of Popes who reigned during the period of St. Augustine:

St. Julius I	337–352
St. Liberius	352–366
St. Damasus I	366–384
St. Siricius	384–399
St. Athanasius I	399–401
St. Innocent I	401–417
St. Zosimus (Greek)	417–418
St. Boniface I	418–422
St. Celestine I	422–432
St. Sixtus III	432–440

Chapter Four

¹ Speech of Symmachus in favor of the restoration of the altar and statue of Victory:

"Who can find fault with us for defending the institutions of our ancestors, the rights and future of the fatherland, with as much energy as we defend the fame of our own century, which will in fact be all the greater if we allow no departure from the customs of our fathers?

"Who could be so friendly to the barbarians as not to demand the restoration of the altar of Victory? If we neglect the goddess, at least let us show respect to her name! Although those who have never known her favors have disdained her powers, this Divinity has been worshiped all over the world, and we must not cease to honor one from whose invocation such great benefits have been derived.

"If respect for Victory exists no longer, at least her altar, so great an ornament to the Curia, should not have been degraded. Respect for custom is an important thing. Before this altar have come our citizens seeking justice before the law; our sentences have never carried such authority as when obedience to them was sworn it. A sacrilegious refuge has therefore been placed at the disposition of the perjurer. And to think this violation was permitted by princes who swore publicly to hold their trust inviolable!

"It seems to me that Rome herself arises before us, and that she speaks to me in these terms:

" 'Father of the Country, respect my old age; you will have no reason to regret it. This cult has roamed the world in accordance with our laws; these mysteries have repulsed Hannibal from our walls. What matters it by what means each one of us pursues his search for Truth? We shall never reach, by one path alone, the solution of this great mystery.'

"The Treasury withholds the legacies willed by the dying to the virgins and the pontiffs. How shall we name this spoliation? It is not the weeds that have smothered our harvests; it is sacrilege that has dried up our fields.

"The Republic is made up of all its citizens and whatever is hers is for the benefit of each individual. Question your own generosity and ascertain if you can refuse to consider as a public good whatever has been dedicated to the glory of Rome."

² "Plotinus said: 'It is in God that the pure soul dwells with the ineffable essences.' Did not Saint Paul call Christ Wisdom, and did not Saint John say, 'In the beginning was the Word'?

"God exists and He is Truth, that is to say, what Plotinus calls Intelligence." *On the Trinity*

[3] "Justice, wisdom, courage and temperance are the mainsprings of Plato's Republic. Neither men's consciences nor States can find true happiness save in obedience to the great moral laws outlined by philosophy; but this obedience, difficult without religion, is impossible without grace." *Letter to Macedonius*

[4] "Plato opposes the world of the senses to that of the Spirit. He tries to rise from the second to the first by an intellectual and moral dialectic. The soul differs from the body and should survive it. A spiritual hierarchy exists at the summit of which we find the supreme good—God." *Soliloquies*

[5] *On Plato*: "He understood that the soul of man, however immortal, reasoning or intellectual it might be, could possess beatitude only to the degree that it participates in the Light of Him who made the world. He maintained that none could attain to the object of every man's desire, namely happiness, without being closely bound to the One Being and Sovereign Good who is no other than the supreme and immutable God.

"Plotinus, in commenting on Plato, declares on several occasions that the soul of the universe has no other principle of happiness than our own and that this principle is a Light to which it owes its being and which fills it with intellectual understanding. In regard to this, he makes a comparison with the celestial bodies in which he likens God to the sun. This great Platonist says that the reasoning soul has no nature higher than itself save God, the author of the universe, and the author of that soul; and that the celestial spirits receive the light of intelligence and truth from no other Source than the one from which we receive it ourselves."

[6] "If I tore my hair, and beat my forehead, if I locked my fingers together and clasped my knees, I did so because I willed it. But I could have willed this and yet not done it, if the motive power of my limbs had not made its response.

"Therefore I did many things in which to will was not the same as the ability to act. Yet I did not do that which I wanted to do with an incomparably greater desire, and could have done as soon as I willed to act, for immediately, when I made that act of will, I would have willed with efficacy. In such an act the power to act and the will itself are the same, and the very act of willing is actually to do the deed.

"Yet is was not done. It was easier for the body to obey the soul's most feeble command, so that its members were moved at

pleasure, than for the soul to obey itself and to accomplish its own
high will wholly within the will." *Confessions*

⁷ "Poor child that I was, when I had to go on with my studies
you received me into your house and, better still, into your heart.
When I wished to go to Carthage to find a more illustrious position
as a teacher, you understood it was useless to oppose the violent
desires of a young man on his way to what seemed to him a better
place in life. With great benevolence you turned your words of warning into promises of support, and furnished me with all I needed for
the journey. When I crossed the sea in your absence you did not
take offense from a silence that was not habitual with me and you
remained unwavering in your friendship. And finally, my freedom to
breathe, to live and to find myself again, my pleasure in seeking after
truth—all these are due to you. My faith, rather than my reason,
has shown me whose minister you are." *Letter to Romanianus*

Chapter Five

¹ "6+1=7, 3×3=9. These propositions are certain. Thus in geometry when we ask ourselves the definition of a straight line or of a circle
we arrive at a certainty about which no doubt can arise.

"Dialectic also leads to certainties which are beyond criticism, and
is subjacent to all science based on what is true. Every regular
discipline, even grammar, is made up of knowledge which is true."
MARROU

² Mathematical truth was to serve him in establishing the spiritual
nature of the soul.

"Have you ever seen with fleshy or material eyes a point, a line,
a surface? Strictly speaking, no. It is because of a *mystical relationship*
that we perceive them. The *animus* with which we see these im-
material elements must be neither material, nor matter.

"Here too the idea of preparing the mind takes on great importance.
It is a rich and fruitful idea of culture and is opposed to the super-
ficial idea of the theorists of the oratorical art."

Augustine revived still another Platonic idea, that of the *awakening*
sciences which prepare the soul for the contemplation of eternal
truth and he describes the role of the various disciplines. The "eye
of the soul" is reason, its sun is God. The rational sciences are
objects which project the eternal light but in a lesser way.

³ Tertullian was the first to propose, in his book *On the Pre-
scription of Heretics* the theory of submission to ecclesiastical law,

a law to which Augustine always gave unconditional obedience. Two principles were dominant in his theology: simplicity and continuity. "All which comes into being is from God," he said, "and all that is artificial comes from the devil. Nature is our first school; what is contrary to nature is monstrous."

Chapter Six

[1] The forty-sixth question of the book *On Eighty-three Different Questions* contains an indication of the direction of Augustine's future system of thought:

"Divine Wisdom only creates what is good and what is reasonable. 'Other things' can only exist outside God. If the reasons for things created or to be created exist in the Divine Mind, those things are eternal and immutable. Nothing that is not eternal or immutable can exist in God. These reasons are not only ideas but truths. All existence is a manner of participating in these reasons or in these truths. Thus each thing has its Idea in God, and is distinct from every other.

"God looks on creation and finds it good. The partial disorder we perceive is seen from a limited point of view—the soldier does not see the disposal of the whole army. This does not mean that evil is eliminated because of this, but all, even disorder, is included in the providential order.

"God created light and not darkness, which is the privation of light. We cannot substitute ourselves for God to decide regarding the usefulness of beings He has created in themselves and not in relationship to us.

"But this is only to evade the problem. There was the *possibility* of Adam's sin. God made it possible for this sin to be committed.

"*Reply*: Man is free. Man can sin because God gave him free will.

"*Question*: But why did God give man fallible liberty? Is not God responsible for this? He might have created a sinless man—would it not have been better had man been born without the liberty to sin?

"*Reply*: Free will is a way to perfection, even if man makes ill use of it. God wills for men to be what they themselves will. He wishes men freely to do what they do. But he did not wish them to do evil.

"*Question*: Does God foresee what will happen?

"*Reply*: No, since everything is present for Him. We use in speaking of Him the same words we apply to men—how can we do otherwise, seeing that we are men? God is not indeterminate. He is conscious of Himself and of His work: He does nothing of which He is unaware. Providence, the Holy Spirit, by which God has created everything, governs all. . . .

"Beings are born and die at intervals, as though these things make up the syllables and words of a marvelous canticle. They are neither longer nor shorter than the requirements of the melody conceived and determined in advance."

² "Just as geometry is not a science of so many numbers traced with a stick in the sand, so music should transcend the sensible charm which derives from its modulation so that we may devote our attention to its mathematical laws. We cannot fail to note in passing the lacuna left in ancient thought by the absence of a notion of art. Ordinarily a rather false idea is held of the role played by music in ancient civilization. The progress of Hellenic civilization led to specialization in music as with almost everything else. The great thinkers of classical times, Plato and Aristotle lived at the period of this musical revolution but determinedly ignored it. Their attitude in regard to musical art is curious if we contrast it with the passionate and informed interest with which Plato and Aristotle followed the scientific developments of their time.

"The divide which separated the experience of musicians from the speculation of the philosophers was never to be filled in. The former continued to devote their attention to music, but the music they were forced to study was no longer the art of the virtuoso, but the *musica* which Saint Augustine defines, an abstract science with no relationship to practice." MARROU

³ "Augustine succeeded in elaborating his celebrated theory of sensation. This elementary form of the life of the spirit is not, as it might seem, the action of matter on a soul that is passive. On the contrary, it is the effect of the soul's activity on the soul itself. It is the consequence of the attention the soul devotes to the affections of the body it animates and to needs for which it is ever on the alert. This doctrine of sensation is a definitive response to the materialism which held Augustine captive for so long during his Manichaean period. We see to what heights a gradual deepening of the notion of rhythm can lead.

"The second part of his book is devoted to an analysis of aesthetic pleasure, and its reduction to philosophical contemplation. In the matter of judging the rhythm of a beautiful poem, Augustine introduces a distinction between the aesthetic judgment that leads us to find this rhythm agreeable and the rational judgment which enables us to pronounce on its nature. What could the activity of reason be here if not to judge, comprehend, and analyze the elements that cause the aesthetic pleasure? This effort leads to the constitution of the rational science which we have called *musica*. Saint Augustine shows it is the fruit of this application of reason to the problems of aesthetic pleasure." MARROU

4 Hippo is now Bône, or rather Bône rose from the ruins of Hippo. Very little is left of the ancient city. There seems to be no trace of the Basilica of Peace where the great bishop preached for more than thirty years. However, remains have been found of the baths made famous by the debate between Saint Augustine and the Manichaean priest Fortunatus.

Saint Augustine is still venerated by the Kabyle inhabitants who refer to him as the "Great Christian," and invoke him for protection against plague and sickness.

Chapter Eight

1 "This program was to be of considerable historical importance. Following the prescriptions of *On Christian Doctrine* and under the aegis of Augustine's great authority, the Christian culture of the Middle Ages developed the values of humanism, the taste for scientific research and that curiosity for knowledge of every kind which, in a word, was to give birth to the culture of modern times. For example, Augustine speaks of having brought to him the fruit of a mandrake, of examining its form, its smell, its taste, in order to clarify a passage of Genesis in which this fruit was the subject of a dispute between Jacob's two wives. He identifies in passing the site of such and such a place, the boundary lines of Egypt, etc.

"The first step in penetrating the meaning of Scripture, he wrote, was to examine the Biblical language under all its aspects, to analyze its verbal forms, to translate obscure passages clearly with frequent reference to the context, and at the same time to consider each verse in itself as filled with valuable meaning.

"But many points in the Bible in Latin, he said, are not understandable unless referred back to the Hebrew. He was therefore forced to do the best he could without knowing Hebrew, to try to infer or divine the precise sense of certain words and to determine the real value of idioms preserved in the Latin version.

"He found his resumption of Greek studies most helpful. The Greek translation helped him to avoid many wrong constructions, clarified obscure passages and ambiguities.

"Saint Augustine made no claim to "edit" the Bible. His aim was to arrive at the fullest possible comprehension of Revelation.

"To his philological knowledge, Saint Augustine added whatever learning he had in the other sciences. For example, the nature of the wind, the phases of the moon, natural history. He also made use of actual happenings and fabulous stories to illustrate his points.

"According to him, mathematics is by far the most valuable science for systematic use. Here the Neoplatonic philosopher, imbued with Pythagorism, comes into his own. Augustine's patristic mathematics adapt this tradition to Christian dogma and the requirements of the Bible. For God is one; three the Trinity; twelve the Apostles; two the charity prescribed by the two commandments; ten, the divine law based on the Decalogue; four, universality, because there are four seasons, four parts of the world, four winds in space; five, the laws contained in the books of Moses; six, a perfect number symbolizing achievement, realization, fullness, one, plus two, plus three; seven, universality, as the meeting of the first odd and the first even; eleven signifying sin, because it goes beyond the law, which is ten, etc.

"The problems of physics and astronomy occupy an important place, an idea borrowed from the great pagan philosophers, notably the Aristotelians—the four elements, etc. If he discusses these questions, it is because anxious souls or malicious pagans have used arguments based on such things to criticize the story of Genesis and the dogmas arising from it.

"His aim is not to add to the natural sciences but to remove objections against faith raised in the name of those sciences. It was important to show the Scripture as neither contradictory nor absurd, and as in accordance with accepted data on the workings of nature.

"Finally, I need not stress Augustine's use of the resources of the dialectical art. It was due to his incomparable mastery of this that he met with such success in his long polemics against the heretics."
MARROU

[2] St. Augustine's sermons, in the Benedictine edition, are divided into four classifications: the first contains 183 sermons on Sacred Scripture; the second, 88 sermons on the principal feasts of the year; the third, 69 sermons on the feasts of the saints; the fourth, 23 sermons on various subjects.

[3] St. Augustine realized, insofar as it lay within his power, the ideal of the Christian orator as he conceived him to be. It is enough to examine carefully any example of this aspect of his literary genius to realize that the art it reveals exactly befits the Doctor of the Church, the exegete, the theologian, the bishop, the pastor. His was

an art of manifold resources, rich and varied in its shadings, capable of adapting itself to the most diverse situations. His eloquence was strong, effective, strictly subordinated in form to content and aim, and therefore of a deeply religious character; an eloquence that fed on the Bible and sacred writers, and was illuminated by his own experiences; moreover, an eloquence that avoided the occasional excesses of other ecclesiastical writers. Augustine was the first to conform in this matter to the requirements which he had laid down for his disciples.

[4] According to Augustine the cause of the downfall of the bad angel was that he had turned away from Him who is Being Itself. Pride is the origin of all sin; human sufferings are explained by this same cause. Adam and Eve are punished in their offspring.

In his *Republic*, Plato says: "God is innocent."

But God knows in advance that Adam would sin. He knew the calamities which would befall mankind because of Adam's sin.

He could do anything. He could create or not create. He could send to him whom He pleased the necessary ideals and feelings to avoid any evil. But in freedom Adam sinned, and it is in freedom that all men sin or else acquire merit by resisting temptation.

Chapter Nine

[1] "He places himself *within* the Bible and discusses neither its inspiration nor its strict veracity. His sole aim is to show it is possible to solve the apparent contradictions it contains, and that our faith in it is completely justified.

"He does not ask the Synoptic Evangelists to furnish him reasons for faith; they are speaking to believers, not to pagans. His only ambition is to show that there is no insoluble contradiction between those narratives and that they may be considered as literally exact, down to the smallest details.

"Book XVIII, of the *City of God*, for instance, is devoted to the religion of Israel and to Christianity from the birth of Abraham to Pentecost, a Sacred History in which all the events are placed in juxtaposition to the events of human history in a careful chronological order. For example, he tells us that Abraham was born during the reign of Ninus, the second king of the Assyrians; that Jesus died the eighth day before the calends of April during the consulate of the two Gemini, etc.

"The Bible has its place at the heart of universal history, and constitutes one of its elements. From its teaching emerges a principle which permits men to judge all history." MARROU

2 "I feel, with all the force of my soul that I am free to will or not to will, to act or not to act. I also feel keenly my weakness toward the Good. Since the corruption of my nature binds or weighs down my wings, I bless the divine Hand that frees them and gives the lightness to raise me up to the regions of virtue. And as the act of Good always carries with it the idea of a victorious struggle against Evil on the part of man, our merits are the result of our interior strength and of our liberty.

"It is not true that grace may be refused to man. Christianity teaches that grace has been granted even to pagans. If Christian society more than any other has given the world examples of high virtue, it is because, under the empire of the Cross, God has visited man more intimately and granted him gifts more magnificent."

The Pelagians held that Adam's sin was personal, that toil and death were not the punishment of the first fall, that human nature today is what it was before the sin of the first man. Now there is no Christian religion that does not believe in original sin and the need for redemption.

The decree of predestination, sprung from the divine mercy, leaves complete freedom to the human will. No one knows without a miraculous revelation whether or not he belongs to the number of the elect. Thus each man should strive to reach the eternal Kingdom.

In healing the soul of man, grace gives him the love of justice and restores the primitive balance of his will. Augustine held that Faith is the gift of God; that all power comes from God, that God imposes no "necessity"; that free will is situated in a sort of middle ground between faith and unbelief. Man may rise to one, or cast himself down into the other. The very will to believe in God springs from the depth of the free will granted man at the moment of his creation, so it can be said that free will and the will to believe come to him from God.

Now, God calls all men to salvation and to the knowledge of truth, but without taking from them that free will whose good or evil use determines the morality of action.

"If someone asks why one man in convinced of the truths preached to him and why the other is not persuaded, there come to my mind but two things to say to him: 'O depths of the riches of the wisdom and knowledge of the Lord, how incomprehensible are His judgments and how unsearchable His ways!' If we wish to explain the justice from on high by the conjectures of our mind, we are building up fables. Christ's liberating and redeeming mission is the only admissible response to all the mysteries of man's destiny." J.J.F. POUJOULAT

Chapter Ten

[1] "Setting forth a general theory of Christian eloquence, Saint Augustine returned to the classical formula of the three aims of the orator: to instruct, to please, to move. He had no difficulty in showing that the aim of religious literature is first to *instruct*. It should *move*, if it is a question of convincing those who hesitate. Should it try to *please?* Yes, in the measure that this is useful to hold the attention of the public.

"The *De Doctrina Christiana* was something new, different from what had hitherto been taught by the classical school, and it bore the mark of Augustine's genius." MARROU

[2] No Father of the Church, except Saint Jerome, made so extensive a study of Judaism as Saint Augustine. In his commentaries on the *Heptateuch*, he made a summary of Hebraic teaching. In his *Sermons* and his explanation of the *Psalms*, he explained the political and social psychology of the people of God, and in the *City of God*, he gave an outline of their history.

Heir to the thought of Saint Ambrose, he wrote that the Jews, the "privileged sons of God," had become the "children of the devil, their religious practices fallen into formalism long before the coming of Christ." But he did not think they should be proscribed: "There were the Prophets, there the Temple was first built, there lived the Patriarchs, and Christ Himself was born of Abraham's race."

Fifteen months before his death he wrote: "We should not rise up in pride before these broken reeds. Let us remember the roots from which we spring. Come, let us march together in the light of the Lord.

"God sent down hard chastisement upon the Jews. He unleashed the Roman legions against Jerusalem. He dispersed them throughout the world. These sad and moving happenings hold a useful lesson for the Christian State. The Jews do not cease to renew their miracles. Their customs, their race, their language and their religion have resisted the political pressure and violence of the alien. What mystery, then, is attached to this people? God does not destroy the character of the Jewish race lest it no longer be able to render its testimony. He made this race the guardian of His Scripture."

Chapter Eleven

1 "The barbarians did not overthrow the Roman Empire of the West. It fell noiselessly and of its own weight like a deck of cards— an immense territory of more than two and a half million square miles, sixty-six million inhabitants and some three hundred thousand soldiers.

"The Vandals needed only twenty thousand men to conquer Africa, a country where the Empire had never sent more than fifteen thousand fighters. Moreover, this army sent by the Romans was recruited from among the barbarians, since the Romans themselves refused military service. One had to speak German in order to understand the last defenders of Rome. Soon the world would see an emperor of the West clothed in the skins of animals, riding at the head of his troops." JEAN DUCHÉ, *Histoire du Monde*

2 "The ancient Romans were feared; we ourselves are fearful. Barbarous peoples paid tribute to them; we pay tribute to the barbarians. These enemies sell us our lives at usurious prices. Almost all our public possessions are being bartered away, and to crown all, we make ourselves ridiculous by calling *largesse* the money we pay! We call *gifts* what are but the price of purchase.

"All prisoners are set at liberty once they have paid ransom. As for ourselves, we go on paying and we are never free." SALVIANUS, *On the Government of God*

3 "The Grecian Graces give place to the deep and mysterious Grace of Paradise, that veiled virgin who comes to every man in the quiet of the evening. Uneasy in mind and with anxious feeling, agitated in thought, imprisoned within a cell when he longed for vast and open spaces, the first great religious mind of modern times cried out ceaselessly in his misery to the Omnipotent God and considered himself unworthy of God's mercy. This satiety with life came from within—it was a yearning *à rebours*. The heart hungered for what it did not have, and vomited forth what it had.

"Thus Saint Augustine initiates us into the anguish of the Christian before the gates of Hell. It was not the rebellion of the unworthy 'Self' before nothingness. He was leading the new man into an immense forest." ANDRÉ SUARÈS

4 *Thoughts of Saint Augustine*

Love alone makes the dividing line between the children of God and the children of the devil.

You think you are doing God a service when you love Him. Be not deceived; in loving God you are the one who draws the benefit.

The doctor drives out the disease and saves the patient. God does the same with sin.

To live the truth is better than preaching. Be the listener. When we are among the listeners we remain humble; when we preach, it is hard to keep a little vanity from slipping into our hearts.

Do not stray far from Christ, the true Man, before you come to the Christ who proceeds only from the Father, the true God.

We should never have been freed from sinful flesh if God had not assumed the likeness of that same sinful flesh.

Bear with the erring. Who was ever always good?

Satan has no power to force us to do what is contrary to our will. He tries to use persuasion.

Virtue is a praiseworthy thing, but if you possess it, tell me whence it came?

The fool has said in his heart: there is no God. But Christ died for sinners.

Fear no enemy but yourself. Conquer yourself and you have conquered the world.

Men run a double danger—that of hoping too much and that of despairing.

We must neither hate vice because of a man nor hate a man because of his vices.

Give praise with your life and not with your tongue, with your deeds and not with sounds.

To be born, to suffer and to die, these are the only wares we find in the markets of the world.

Judas' misfortune was his despairing conviction that he would never obtain mercy.

On this cross, Jesus healed your wounds by making them His own.

If you throw your sin behind you, God himself will place it again before your eyes.

Christ's weakness is our strength.

Christ condemned the sin, not the sinner.

You are afraid of an evil death, but you do not fear to live an evil life.

BIBLIOGRAPHY

WORKS ON ST. AUGUSTINE

Alfaric, P., *Evolution intellectuelle de saint Augustin*, 1918

Allard, Paul, *Le Christianisme et l'Etat romain*, 1890

Allin, T., *The Augustinian Revolution in Theology*, 1911

Altheim, *Le déclin du monde antique*

Batiffol, P., *Le catholicisme de saint Augustin*, 1921

Bertrand, Louis, *Autour de saint Augustin*, 1921

——*Celle qui fut amie d'Augustin*, 1935

    St. Augustine. Trans. by Vincent O'Sullivan, 1914

Bloch, G., *L'Empire romain* (n.d.)

Boissier, G., *La fin du paganisme*, 1891

——*L'Afrique romaine*, 1895

Bourke, Vernon J., *Augustine's Quest of Wisdom*, 1945

Boyer, C., *Christianisme et néoplatonisme dans la formation de saint Augustin*, 1920

——*L'Idée de Vérite chez saint Augustin*, 1920

Carcopino, G., *Daily Life in Ancient Rome*, 1960

Cayre, F., *Principes de la spiritualité de saint Augustin*, 1920

Combes, Gustave, *La doctrine politique de saint Augustin*, 1925

——*Saint Augustin et la culture classique*, 1927

Courcelle, P., *Histoire littéraire des invasions*, 1950

——*Recherches sur les Confessions de saint Augustin*, 1950

Cresson, André, *Saint Augustin*, 1958

Cunningham, W., *St. Austin, and His Place in the History of Christian Thought*, 1886

Daniel-Rops, H., *The Church in the Dark Ages*, 1959

——*The Church of Apostles and Martyrs*, 1960

D'Arcy, M. C., and others, *A Monument to St. Augustine*, 1930

Delastre, L. A., *Sainte Monique*, 1959

Demongeot, E., *De l'unité à la division de l'Empire*, 1936

Fabre, Lucien, *Saint Augustin*, 1951

Fleury, A., *Politique chrétienne de saint Augustin*, 1730

Gilson E., *Introduction à l'étude de saint Augustin*, 2d ed., 1943
———*Christian Philosophy of St. Augustine*, 1960
Gosselin, B.-Rolland, *La morale de saint Augustin*, 1925
Grandgeorge, *Saint Augustin et le néoplatonisme*, 1896
Gsell, H., *Algérie dans l'antiquité*, 1900
———*Histoire de l'Algérie*, 1927
Hatzfeld, Ad., *St. Augustine*. Trans. E. Holt, 1898
Jolivet, Régis, *Le problème du mal chez saint Augustin*, rev. ed. 1937
Leclercq, Henri, O.S.B., *L'Afrique chrétienne*, 2 vols., 1904
Marrou, Henri, *St. Augustine and His Influence through the Ages*.
    Trans. Patrick Hepburne-Scott, 1957
———*Saint Augustin et la fin de la culture antique*, 1950
———*Saint Augustin et l'augustinisme*, 1955
Martin, Jules, *Doctrine spirituelle de saint Augustin*, 1903
Mommsen, Theodor, *History of Rome*, 5 vols., 1854–85
Monceaux, Paul, *Histoire littéraire de l'Afrique chrétienne*, 1923
Montgomery, W., *St. Augustine: Aspects of His Life and Thought*,
    1914
Morgan, J., *The Psychological Teaching of St. Augustine*, 1932
Nebreda, *Bibliographia Augustiniana*, 1930
Nourrisson, Jean-Félix, *La philosophie de saint Augustin*, 1863
O'Meara, J., *The Young Augustine: the Growth of St. Augustine's
    Mind up to His Conversion*, 1954
Papini, Giovanni, *St. Augustine*. Trans. Mary P. Agnetti, 1930
Picavet, F., *Hypotases plotiniennes et Trinité chrétienne*, 1907
Piganiol, A., *L'Empire chrétien*, 1947
Pope, Hugh, O.P., *St. Augustine of Hippo*, 1949
Possidio, *Vita de S. Agostino; a cura de M. Pellegrino*, 1955
Poujoulal, J.J.F., *Vie de saint Augustin*, 1943
Pryzwara, E., *An Augustine Synthesis*, 1936
Stein, Ernest, *Histoire du Bas Empire*, 1959
Suarès, André, *Martyre de saint Augustin*, 1929
Thanun, *Saint Ambroise et la morale chrétienne au IVe siècle*, 1895
Tillemont, Lenain de, *Mémoires pour servir à l'histoire ecclésiastique
    des six premiers siècles*, 1686
Van der Meer, F., *Augustine the Bishop*, 1962
Villemain, A., *Tableau de l'éloquence chrétienne au IVe siècle*, 1836
Wohl, Louis de, *Saint Augustine*, 1955
Zeller, E., *Quelques fleurs du jardin de saint Augustin*

NOTE:
There has been no complete translation of all the works of St.

Augustine into English. On the other hand there have been many translations of separate works either individually or as parts of various Patristic series.

In recent years, works of St. Augustine have appeared in English translations in the following series: The Catholic University of America Patristic Studies (Washington, D.C., 1922–); Ancient Christian Writers: The Works of the Fathers in Translation (Newman Press, Westminster, Maryland and Longmans, London, 1946–); The Library of Christian Classics (London, 1953–); and The Fathers of the Church (New York, 1947). In addition to the translations appearing in these series, there are separate translations of individual works, collections of translations of a number of works (such as Whitney J. Oates, *Basic Writings of Saint Augustine*, New York, 1948), and translations of individual works appearing in other series (such as the *Confessions* and *Select Letters* in the Loeb Classical Library).

PRINCIPAL WORKS
OF ST. AUGUSTINE

	On the Work of Monks (*De Opere monachorum*)
400	Against Faustus, the Manichaean (*Contra Faustum Manichaeum*)
	Confessions (*Confessionum Libri Tredecim*)
400–02	Against the Letters of Petilianus (*Contra Litteras Petiliani*)
401	On Marriage (*De Bono Conjugali*)
401–15	Genesis (*De Genesi ad Litteram*)
405	On the Nature of Good (*De Natura Boni*)
c. 405–11	Letter to Emeritus
408	Two Letters to Olympius
	Letter to Vincent the Rogatist
409	Letter to the Donatists
410	On Single Baptism (*De Unico Baptismo*)
	Sermons on the Sack of Rome
410 or 411	Letter to Dioscorus
411	Discourse on Peace
	Sermons against the Pelagians
412	Treatise on the Punishment and Remission of Sin (*De Peccatorum Meritis et Remissione*)
	The Spirit and the Letter (*De Spiritu et Litteras*)
413	City of God (*De Civitate Dei*, first part)
	Faith and Works (*De Fide et Operibus*)
415	On Nature and Grace (*De Natura et Gratia*)
416	Sermons on the First Epistle of Saint John (*Tractatus Decem in Epistolam Joannis ad Parthos*)
	On the Trinity (*De Trinitate*, end)
417–27	Four Letters to Boniface
418	Against Pelagius and Coelestius (*Contra Pelagium et Coelestium, De gratia Christi . . .*)
	Discourse in Caesarea on Catholic Unity (*Sermo ad Caesareensis Ecclesiae Plebem*)
419–20	On Marriage and Concupiscence (*De Nuptiis et Concupiscentiis*)
	On the Origin of the Soul (*De Anima et ejus Origine*)
c. 421	Against Julian and the Pelagians (*Contra Julianum Haeresis Pelagianae Defensorem*)
424	Letters against the Semi-Pelagians (*Contra Duas Epistolas Pelagianorum*)
426	On Christian Doctrine (*De Doctrina Christiana*, end)
	City of God (*De Civitate Dei*, end)
426–27	On Grace and Free Will (*De Gratia et Libero Arbitrio*)
	Retractations (*Retractationes*)